The Economics of Education

Samuel Akinyemi, PhD

Strategic Book Publishing and Rights Co.

Strategic Book Publishing and Rights Co.
12620 FM 1960, Suite A4-507
Houston TX 77065
www.sbpra.com

ISBN: 978-1-61204-200-8

In Honor of
Professor Tunde Samuel

Professor of economics of education, consultant to the UNESCO on educational costs, and former special adviser on education to the Lagos State Government.

Preface and Acknowledgements

Economics of education as a field of study is relatively new development. It is a discipline that uses a lot of concepts in economics to explain issues in education so as to ensure functionality, efficiency, and effectiveness at all levels of any educational system.

The Economics of Education has been written to provide a vade mecum for both the undergraduate and postgraduate students undertaking their formal course in economics of education. It is also intended for people who actually run formal educational systems and non-formal educational programs, and for those who practice planning, decision-making, and management every day.

The coverage of the subject matter is extensive, but the presentation has been condensed into simple form for ease of comprehension. It is the belief of the author that this book will be of special value to educational managers and administrators, educational planners, teachers, and students of economics of education, as well as to policy makers in the education sector.

I am sincerely grateful to my lecturer and PhD supervisor, Professor Tunde Samuel, whose ideas and lectures have formed parts of this book.

My special gratitude goes to my wife Harriet and to all of my children for giving me motivation and support during the process of writing this book.

Finally, bear in mind that this book makes no claim to having the last word on the subject matter. Economics of education is a dynamic field where new concepts and techniques are constantly being devised, debated, and tested. Those who wish to dig more deeply into the subject should not hesitate to do so.

September 2010

Samuel Akinyemi, PhD
Department of Educational Management,
Lagos State University,
Lagos, Nigeria.

Contents

Chapter One

Economics of Education as a Discipline

Economics of Education Defined

The economics of education is a specialized field of study that applies the principles of economics to education. It has an imitational hypothesis behind its study because it uses a lot of concepts in economics to explain issues in education. As a dynamic discipline, it is primarily concerned with the need for rational decision making in education or the logic of ends and means in educational investment.

Defining the economics of education directly can be vividly understood by first conceptualizing the terms *economics* and *education.*

> Economics is the science that studies the logic, tools, and techniques of making optimum use of the available scarce resources to achieve the given ends.

Lionel Robinson, in his modern definition, describes it as the science that studies human behaviors as the relationship between ends and scarce means, which have alternative uses. Economics is the scientific study of people and their institutions from the point of view of how they go about producing and consuming goods and services, and how they face the problem of making choices in a world of scarce resources. In general, economics is particularly concerned with consumption, production, and resource use by individuals and groups, and with the processes by which decisions about the use of scarce resources are made.

> Education, on the other hand, is an act or a process of providing people with knowledge, skill, competence, and possession of desirable qualities by a formal course of study, institution, or training.

It is the process by which cognitive, affective, and psychomotor faculties of individuals and groups are developed so that they can become useful to themselves and to the society at large. It is also seen as a process through which knowledge and skill values are added to human society to acquire modernization.

Education is a nonmaterial good that is being rendered to satisfy the educational needs of individuals and communities. Consequently, educational resources must be optimally utilized to achieve the educational ends. The logic, the tools, and the techniques of optimum use or utilization of these educational resources to achieve the educational ends are the focus of the economics of education. Thus, the economics of education is the science of allocating scarce educational resources among competing alternatives to education in order to achieve its goals. It is the science that deals with rationalization of scarce educational resources to achieve optimal goals of education. In the area of educational finance, economics of education attempts to find answers to the following nagging fiscal and policy issues:

1. Which education to finance and why?
2. What component of education consumed by individuals constitutes the residual in the economic development?
3. Who should bear the greater cost of education?

4. Should the principle of prime beneficiary or fiscal justice be used to allocate costs in education without reference to different socioeconomic factors?
5. What should influence fiscal sectoral allocation to education in a developing country?
6. What is the symbiotic relationship between educational investment and economic growth?
7. What determines the technical or economic efficiency in educational investment?

Economics of education provides logical and plausible answers to these questions to enable decision makers take rational investment decision in education.

Economics of education covers several areas such as funding of education, educational costs, manpower planning, human capital development, educational investment, cost-benefit analysis, rate of returns, efficiencies in education among others.

Some Basic Concepts in the Economics of Education

Some of the basic concepts that are frequently used in economics of education are as follows:

Per Capita Income

This is the income that is sometimes referred to as the income per person of a country's population. Mathematically, this is calculated as the national income in a particular year divided by the population for that year.

Thus, per capita income $= \frac{\text{National Income (Y)}}{\text{Population (P)}}$

For example:

Table 1.1 Population and National income of two countries in 1990

Countries	National Income	Population	Per Capita Income
Jamaica	$800,000,000	800,000	$1000
Cameroun	$100,000,000	2,000,000	$500

From the illustration above, it can be stated that the average contribution of each person to the national income is higher in Jamaica. Thus, the average output is higher in Jamaica. Given this assertion, it can be said that economic development is higher in Jamaica than in Cameroon. For this reason, per capita income is a better index of economic growth.

National Income

This is the market value or monetary value of all goods and services produced in an economy during a particular year.

National income can be measured in various ways, but the two most frequently used measurements are those of the gross national product (GNP) and the gross domestic product (GDP). While GNP takes into account the total value of all goods and services produced by indigenes of a particular country, home, and abroad (net income from abroad) in a particular year, GDP takes into account the total value of all goods and services produced by both indigenes and non-indigenes in a country during a particular year.

National income helps to determine the wealth of a nation and can thus be used as an index of economic development and growth of the nation.

Growth Rate

This is the change in any measure of development over a period of time. This change can be positive (increase) or negative (decrease). We can talk about growth rates of NI and population, which are very relevant to economics of education.

Income Growth Rate

Income growth rate by formula is IGR $= \frac{Y_n - Y_o}{Y_o} \times 100\%$

Where Y_n = income in period n, (target year) and Y_o = income in period o (base year).

Note

Base year is the beginning of the period under study, while the target year is the end of the period. For example, assuming that in 1987 the NI of Jamaica was $70 million, and in 1989 it was $80 million. Then the income growth rate was 14.3 percent for the three-year period. That is,

$$\frac{\$80 \text{ million} - \$70 \text{ million}}{\$70 \text{ million}} \times \frac{100\%}{1}$$

$$= \frac{\$10 \text{ million}}{\$70 \text{ million}} \times \frac{100\%}{1}$$

$$= 14.3\%$$

Population Growth Rate (PGR)

This has to do with the change in the population of a country over a period of time. It is the rate at which a population is increasing or decreasing in a given year due to certain factors such as birth, deaths, and migrations.

By formula:

$$PGR = \frac{P_n - P_o}{P_o} \times \frac{100\%}{1}$$

Where P_n = Population in period n (target year), and P_o = Population in period o (base year).

For example, assuming the population of Nigeria was 750,000,000 in 1970 and it grew to 800,000,000 in 1973, we can say that the population rate of Nigeria over the period 1970–1973 was 6.6 percent. This is obtained as follows:

$$PGR = \frac{800 \text{ million} - 750 \text{ million}}{750 \text{ million}} \times \frac{100\%}{1}$$

$$= \frac{50,000}{750,000} \times \frac{100}{1} = 6.6\%$$

Physical and Human Capital

Physical capital refers to the acquisition of machinery, monetary resources, and raw materials for further productive uses. Human capital, on the other hand, refers to the stock of educated people who have acquired knowledge and skills through education and training and are at the same time using these knowledge and skills for productive purpose. Both physical and human capitals are catalysts for productivity, which eventually lead to economic growth and development. It is human capital in particular that accounts for a significant proportion of the residual or unexplained part of economic growth.

Consumption and Investment

Consumption refers to the purchase of a good or service that gives utility (immediate satisfaction) to the person purchasing it. Investment, on the other hand, is a present sacrifice that will lead to a future flow of satisfaction. Investment, in other words, refers to the production or purchase of a good or service that will provide future satisfaction for a long period.

Demand and Supply

Demand refers to the quantity of a given commodity or service that a person is willing to buy for a given price and at a given point in time. The demand for education, for instance, is a function of its price, utility, and the ability of government and people to pay for it.

Supply, on the other hand, refers to the quantity of a commodity or service a producer is willing to put in the market over a given period of time at a given price. The supply of education, for instance, is a function of the fiscal strength of the government and private educational investors as well as the relevance or utility of education to the economy and society.

Expenditure and Cost

Expenditure refers to the amount of resources that is directly spent by a producer or consumer in the process of producing or purchasing a good or service. Expenditure can be expressed in two broad ways in economics of education:

Current and Capital Expenditures

While current expenditure (recurrent expenditure) is the money outlay on goods and services that bring short lived benefits—usually for not more than one year—capital expenditure is the money spent on buildings and equipment which have a long life span and produce benefits or services over a period of many years. In the case of current expenditure, the length of life is usually not more than a year, while in the case of capital expenditure, it is more than a year.

Cost

Cost is the money expended or sacrifice made on a good or service by an individual or government or institution. Cost is usually categorized into private and social costs. Private cost is the money incurred by individuals, while social cost is the money expended by the government or community.

Efficiency and Productivity

Efficiency refers to the capacity of a system to turn its product with minimum wastage. In other words, it connotes the ability to produce or achieve a desired end with minimum effort or resources used.

Productivity is the relationship between the cost of producing outputs in a particular period, and the cumulative benefits (private and social, economic and noneconomic benefits) that subsequently accrue from these outputs over a longer period. It is defined as the ratio of output to input measured in monetary or physical terms.

An educational system can have high internal efficiency yet low external productivity. This happens, for example, when an educational system spends its time and resources efficiently teaching the wrong things that are not relevant to students' needs and the society.

Inputs and Outputs

Inputs refer to the various resources and elements required to enable a system to function. They include not only students, teachers, and managers, but also instructional materials, physical facilities, equipment, and supplies of various sorts. Outputs, on the other hand, refer to the acquired learning skills, insights, attitudes, and styles of thinking that students carry away from the educational system beyond what they brought to it initially. In other words, the outputs are the educational values added to the students by their exposure to the particular educational process.

Cost-Benefit Analysis (CBA)

This is an investment appraisal tool used in determining the yield or return to any investment project. It involves assessing the cost of the project, the expected benefits from the project, and comparing the costs with the benefits to determine the return to the project.

When the return is obtained, the profitability of the project is determined. If the yield or return is greater, then we say the investment is worthwhile, but if it is not, then we say that it is not worthwhile.

Rate of Return

Rate of return refers to the yield or benefit of an investment project. The appropriate rate of return measures the value of an investment to the individuals, the governments, and the community. This value is compared to the cost of the project, which is the opportunity cost of the funds invested in education.

Private Rate of Return

This refers to the yield or benefit accruable to individuals from an investment project. It is the return that measures the relationship between after-tax earning differentials associated with the level of education acquired and those costs that are borne by the individual in educational institution.

Social Rate of Return

This refers to the yield or benefit accruable to state, country, or community for an investment project. It is the measure of economic profitability of an investment expenditure by the state, country, or community.

Internal Rate of Return (IRR)

This refers to the rate of discount that equates the discounted present value of expected benefits and the present value of costs. It is, therefore, the expected earning rate of an investment. Its major application in the evaluation of capital expenditure projects is to decide whether these capital projects offer a satisfactory return to the investor.

Discounting

This is the process by which a future amount of money is converted into its present value. In other words, it is the process through which a rate of interest is used to discount the future value of money.

Age-Earning Profile

In a contemporary economic term, age-earning profile refers to the likely stream of income over the working lifetime of an individual.

Externalities

These are spillover effects that affect society at large positively or negatively without compensation as a result of production or consumption of a good or service by a unit in the economy. In other words, an externality exists when the production or consumption of a good or service by an individual or organizational unit has a direct positive or negative effect on the welfare of the producers or consumers in another organizational or economic unit without compensation.

Effectiveness

This implies optimizing goals. It represents output or achieving desired ends as maximally as possible.

Residual Knowledge

This refers to the skill or expertise labor force acquired through education and training that accounts for a significant proportion of unexplained economic growth in a particular country.

Market Votes and Political Votes

Market votes are preferences in a competitive market place. They are the preferences acquired by individuals in a competitive market place based on the level of individuals' incomes. These votes are allocated differently between individuals. Those with larger incomes have more market votes compared to those with smaller incomes. Compare this to a democratic political voting system in which each man has one vote, regardless of his income. Political votes postulate one man receives one vote irrespective of his income. This encourages the principles of equity or distribution justice, while market votes posit that individual consumers' preferences should be weighed and allocated by their market power (incomes). Political votes postulate that the democratic political preferences should be allocated equally to individuals regardless of their levels of income.

Chapter Two

Education, Jobs and Income

Education

Education plays a central role in modern labor markets in that to qualify for work most times, workers need special knowledge, skills, or training that economists call the human capital. Education is one of the major means through which individuals acquire the abilities, skills, and knowledge needed to enable them function effectively in the labor markets. In other words, the knowledge and skills acquired through education enhance their productivity, which to a large extent determines wages.

It is widely accepted that a positive relationship exists between education and the labor market. Several studies completed in different countries at different times have confirmed that individuals with higher levels of education earn higher incomes (wages), are easily employed, and work in more prestigious occupations than their counterparts with lower levels of education.

Education and Jobs

In most jobs, a worker is expected to have acquired some skills before being considered for employment. According to human capital theory, there is a causal chain from training/education to employability and wages (income).

Human capital theorists advocate that individuals, parents, governments, and the society at large should invest in human beings through education and training, and this process of schooling equips the individuals with knowledge and skills that make them productive and yield benefits in the future in the form of better employability and higher salaries.

Education and jobs can be viewed from two different perspectives:

Increased Productivity

Individuals with higher levels of education have higher degrees of productive capacities and more efficiency in employment searches. The level of productivity of the individuals determines the probability for better employments and higher pay.

At macro level, the correlation between education and employment has significant effects on the economy in that increase in the employment of individuals with more education will lead to increase in income per capita and national income.

Accuracy of Education

Education helps the supply of workforce to adapt to the labor demand by ensuring that the curriculum contents of courses offered in the educational institutions respond to the working needs of the society. In other words, the right education (meeting societal aspirations/goals) will provide the right workforce in response to the labor demand and this will in turn make for easier employment. The acquisition of the right kind of education by individuals occurs throughout their lifespan to when they actively participate in the labor market by way of employment. The quality of education acquired enhances their level of productivity and their chances of employability.

At the lower levels of schooling, the relationship between human capital and employment can be said to be mutual in that the effects of education on jobs are equally divided between the gains in wage rate and the gains in employment stability. In this connection, Heitala (2006) posits that basic education defines the nature of the future career of individuals and affects their future employability.

The Screening Hypothesis and Employability

The screening hypothesis postulates that to select workers, adequate screening is necessary in order to recruit the best in terms of the competence needed for the job. In job selection circles, therefore, employers scrutinize the certificates of applicants believing that certificates are true evidence of individuals' competency attainment. The possibility of a worker to be employed depends on the acquisition of academic qualifications.

The assumption of this theory is premised on the notion that the residual knowledge of an unschooled or uneducated person is 0.0 alpha coefficient, (proportion of a person's premium that reflects education), meaning that this person does not have any useful productive skill. On the other hand, the residual knowledge of an educated person is put at 0.66 alpha coefficient. This means that the average person who has acquired education has above average competency level to utilize in productive employment.

The hypothesis is a theory of credentialism, which stresses that certificated workers will have inherent ability to perform well on the job with minimum supervision. The higher the academic qualification of an individual, the more able he is to get a better employment with more attractive remuneration in comparison with his counterpart with a lower qualification.

The Problems of the Screening Hypothesis

The hypothesis that examination is not the true test of knowledge is in agreement with the statement that knowledge is different from certificate. Some individuals did all they could to cheat in examinations and eventually came up with good grades. It was later discovered that the ability to perform and defend these grades was not there. Yet, based on the screening hypothesis, these people are qualified for better placement.

Circumstantial factors such as death of a dear one, sickness, restlessness, and similar issues may not allow an individual to perform well in an examination. People so affected are screened out irrespective of their latent potentials. If the screening is for certificates, the best workers may have been left out.

The screening model can also be faulted for not identifying what should be done with those people that are screened out for lacking the object for the exercise.

Despite its negative implications, the screening model helps manpower planners to ensure that as much as possible only the best are trained, recruited, and employed

The Invisible Handshake and Employability

The invisible handshake is an economic theory developed by Adam Smith (1776) in *The Wealth of Nations*. He opines that as individuals pursue their own interests, they would be led as if by an invisible hand "an invisible hand" to promote the good of the society. That is, an individual by pursuing his own interests frequently promotes those of the society more effectually than he really intends to do.

Adam Smith, relating the invisible handshake to education, postulates that there is an intangible, intensive, aesthetic, and sometimes romantic relationship between the prospects that are accruable in education and their benefits in general. The invisible handshake theory sees education as investment and engine room to stimulate and complement positively other sectors of the nation.

What the invisible handshake theory postulates in a nutshell is that an individual that acquires education to better himself in terms of good living, a better job, and an increase in status will promote standard of living in the society indirectly if he is fully employed. That means that the society is benefiting from his education, even when the society did not contribute in training him. The service he is rendering in his workplace is beneficial to the society at large. It is, therefore, erroneous to assume that the human capital is the only factor in the growth process rather it has to interact with other key variables in the causal chain of growth and development.

The Incomplete Contract Theory and Employability

The incomplete contract could be described as a phenomenon that adopts employer-hiring behavior to test the educational signaling hypothesis. It refers to the inability to present academic qualification that an individual claims to possess in his quest for employment. To this extent, there is an incomplete contract between education and the assumed expected benefits that are accruable from education in terms of employment opportunities and better standards of living.

Education is expected to bring some positive changes in individuals and society at large. These changes will include better leadership, good followership, higher societal values, and ethical norms. If individuals fail to exhibit these traits, it could be viewed as an incomplete contract. This is based on the fact that the educational input in terms of knowledge is expected to equilibrate output in terms of changes in behavior.

Education and Income

Education plays an important role in determining the level and distribution of income in the society, productivity, and economic growth.

The positive relationship between education and income (earnings) is universal, and several researchers have confirmed the notion that the investment in education is the key determinant of income. According to Walker and Zhu (2003), education does not only increase the probability of the educated people gaining employment, but the better educated people earn more than their less educated peers when employed.

Hill, Hoffman, and Rex (2005) affirm that individual earnings are directly related to their educational attainment. This difference in the income of individuals based on their levels of education is called earnings differential. The question that always arises on the notion that education increases earnings is , "How much higher is the income of the educated more than that of the less educated?" Price Water House Coppers (2003) opines that the earning gaps between individuals with different levels of educational qualifications are driven by personal characteristics.

Factors Affecting Income Differentials

Some of the factors affecting earning differentials in the labor markets are

- The real demand for supply of labor
- Trade union bargaining power
- Type/nature of the labor market and job
- Choice of academic training
- Level of educational attainment
- Human capital requirement
- Differences in ability and social background
- Experience (years on the job)
- On-the-job training
- Rank
- Rural versus urban locations

Market Demand and Supply of Labor

Forces of supply and demand interact to determine a structure of wages and earnings. These forces also reflect the willingness of labor to supply themselves to various jobs on the offer and the willingness of employers to pay workers for their marginal products. Any deviation from this equilibrium will cause a movement of labor from jobs where wages are too low to jobs where they are too high in order to attain an equilibrium level; therefore, the higher the demand for human capital, the higher the wages bills .

Trade Union Bargaining Power

Labor unions represent the collective interests of their members. Unions have many functions, one of which includes pressing for better and safer working conditions with a major objective of raising members' pay. This implies that those employed in the union sectors will earn higher wages than those employed in the non-union sectors of the economy. Higher union wages are contrary to employers' interests, but they are often forced to agree to the union's higher wage demand. The union has the power to strike and this may result in the employer losing productivity in the process.

Type of Job or the Nature of the Labor Market

The type of market in which labor sells its product can create the difference in the earnings of employees. For instance, employees earn higher wages in union markets than in non-union markets. In a like manner, different types of job attract different wages. For instance, bankers, doctors, and engineers, earn more than gardeners, commercial drivers, and cleaners. This is because the labor market places a higher social value on professional skills than other skills, although all skills are important and complementary.

In relation to the nature of the job, the more risky, unpleasant, and unattractive the job is, the higher the wages paid. Generally, few people are willing to take jobs with higher risks or unpleasant working conditions. For this reason, employers of labor compensate the employees by paying them higher wages. This may in turn attract more workers.

Choice of Academic Training

The type of schooling chose places different individuals at different levels of schooling (Sung, 2005). Differences in the choice of courses and qualifications made by different individuals have led to different amount of consumption benefits. These different qualifications provide different combinations of wages and non-financial returns.

Level of Educational Attainment/Human Capital Requirements

People differ with respect to their training and skills acquired, thereby possessing different levels of educational attainments, which in turn influence wages. Skilled workers are associated with higher marginal productivity and are therefore paid higher wages.

The more the skills acquired by individuals, the higher the demand for this skilled labor, and the higher the income. In other words, the higher the educational attainment, the higher the income. For instance, university degree holders earn higher incomes than the primary school certificate holders do.

Differences in ability and social background

Human beings are different in all respects (personal characteristics). Some have translated their innate attributes into valuable skills. Individuals with greater natural ability are self-motivated and tend to do better than those who are less talented. In other words, talented employees tend to earn higher wages than the less talented ones in the same job. However, there are exceptional cases where some talented employees may prefer to work where their talents are valued, but with less pay especially if there are non-monetary benefits attached.

Job Experience

The pay scale often reflects number of years on the job such that those with longer experiences earn higher wages than those with less experience on the same job.

On-The-Job Training

Workers who have more training on the job are paid more than those with less training are. It is expected that the training will produce more knowledge and skills on the one trained and will improve his productivity. The wage paid in the labor markets is a function of productivity.

Rank

Individuals who are employed at the same time in a particular firm may not necessarily earn the same wages due to the differences in their qualifications and ranks at entry level. Workers with higher qualifications are placed at higher ranks and earn higher incomes than those lower ranks.

Rural/Urban Locations

The location of the firm is also a major determinant of the differences observed in the wages of employers. Individuals working in urban areas earn more than their counterparts working in rural areas do. The reason is that the cost of living and transportation is generally higher in urban areas than rural areas such that employers tend to pay their employees higher wages and benefits in urban areas than rural areas.

In some exceptional cases, those who work in rural areas earn more than their counterparts in urban areas do because of inadequate infrastructural facilities in rural areas. As a way of compensation, the employers pay higher to rural workers to encourage them to stay in rural areas.

Chapter Three

Investment Theory in Education

What is Investment?

The term investment has been conceptualized by different scholars at one time or the other. Investment, according to Small, (1967: 9) is "to incur expenditure now which it is anticipated will produce a stream of benefits which will result in the firm being in a more favorable position than it would have been, and had the original expenditure being directed towards another use."

From this context, individuals and governments invest in projects because of the future benefits that are inherent in them.

In the words of Lucy (1980: 29), "Investment is the process of postponing immediate consumption in the expectation of greater consumption in the future."

Lucy contends that investment entails giving up one thing for another with the hope of acquiring possible benefits later. Investment is regarded as a present sacrifice for future benefits. In other words, investment is what is being offered now in order to have a future stream of benefits. It is an act or activity of giving up a benefit presently enjoyed in order to gain streams of benefits in the future. If applied to education, it implies the building up of future gains in productivity after making some initial expenditure in form of tuition, fees, and other expenses needed for the acquisition of certain skills or knowledge.

The Investment Theory in Education

Investment theory is the ideology that guides a government or an individual to make decisions to put his money, time, and energy where it is felt the benefits will be greater than the costs. The investment theory in education posits that governments or individuals should invest in educational projects with greatest utility or highest rate of returns. Given the investment theory, investment in education is a function of the demand for educated labor and the rate of expansion of aggregate output in the economy (Samuel, 1990). Samuel stresses further that investment decision making in education is a function of the potential contribution to economic growth of the education that is embodied in the labor force.

The investment theory in education proffers that each level of education should witness varied commitment and allocation of resources based on the profitability criterion. For example, if vocational education is going to be more profitable than basic education, then more money should go towards vocational education.

Furthermore, the investment theory in education emphasizes employability of the product of the school system to ensure that the end justifies the means. In a nutshell, investment theory in education postulates that before any investment is made in education, it is very important to determine its worth. This can be done by comparing the streams of expected benefits with the costs of undertaking the investment. In other words, profitability of any investment in education must be considered before embarking on the investment.

Adedeji (2002), posits that investment theory has added a new dimension to the worth of any investment. According to him, the new dimension sees uncertainty, irreversibility, and flexibility as important factors for determining whether or not to invest. Adedeji (2002: 21), stressing these factors, says the following:

"Uncertainty means that investors may fail to invest where there is a high degree of uncertainty and doubt about future returns.

Irreversibility involves sunk cost, which if spent on investments, cannot be recovered after the initial investment, hence this calls for taking a look before one leaps.

Flexibility refers to the timing of investment in order to know the right time to invest because of the risk involved.

These three factors reveal that it is possible for people to fail to invest even when the investment appraisal criteria are met."

Returns to Investment in Education

Returns to investment in education are benefits derived by educational consumers as a result of their investments in education. Educational investment benefits derived by graduates or their parents are referred to as personal/private benefits while educational investment benefits derived by government or society are referred to as social benefits.

Private Returns to Investment in Education

By private returns to investment in education, we mean those benefits accrued to individuals at the end of schooling as a result of investment in education. Whatever benefits a person derives from education belong to the use of that particular person alone. In other words, when outputs of education are felt immediately on a personal level in terms of changed behaviors, attributes, or increased earnings, we regard these as private returns to investment in education.

The private returns to investment in education are numerous; some of these are the following:

Personal Satisfaction

Education gives personal satisfaction. Some people study as a way of spending their leisure time. They study just for their pleasure and satisfaction without any economic motive.

Better Family Life

Education fosters better family life. With education, parents can plan their family size better and understand and play their roles effectively as parents or as husband and wife. There will be more effective communication, ability to resolve conflicts, and in fact more effective management of each other and their growing children. There will be better use of time and family resources to meet the needs of the family.

Children will be properly guided and counseled on issues such as moral and religious education, personal hygiene, career choice, choice of friends, and peer group, interpersonal relationships, decision making, character training, respect and value for life and properties and in fact, prepare them for effective integration into the society.

Self-Development

Education affords a person opportunities for self-education. It refines an individual and broadens his outlook to life. It stimulates his mental activity, makes him inquisitive, think, and act rationally.

Increased Innovative Ability

Whatever an educated person does, he does it better than the uneducated person does, be it tailoring, hairdressing, or buying and selling. His entrepreneurial competence and his innovative ability will make it distinct from the one run by the uneducated person. Take farming for instance; the educated person is likely to be a more aggressively innovative farmer than the uneducated person is. He would seek out useful knowledge, use modern farming inputs more intensively, and in general be more commercially oriented.

Income Earning Potential and Higher Standard of Living

Education affects the income earning potential of individuals and consequently raises the standard of living in their families.

The higher the qualification of a person, the higher the opportunities of getting a lucrative job are. More often than not, highly paid jobs require highly trained personnel. Experts, specialists, and professionals are being sought both within and outside the country. Such jobs usually go with higher pay and higher fringe benefits, which in turn raise the standard of living of families. In this case, post-earnings, which represent the benefit accruable to private household or the individual consumer of education, are accounted for.

Better Social Studies

Education enables people to attain a better status in life. In African countries, lawyers, doctors, and administrators rank higher in public esteem than other professions. They can assume leadership positions that command respect in the society.

More Effective Community Participation

The educated person is an asset to his community. By virtue of his educational training, he is better able to participate more effectively in the life of the community in which he lives. He is able to assist in clarifying issues for better understanding and better reasoning, thereby arriving at better decisions for the benefit of the communities in particular and the nation in general.

Ability to Read and Write

The first and most important benefit of education to an individual is the ability to read and write. An educated person can easily put down his thoughts on paper, as well as read others' ideas on paper; however, the extent to which the educated ones make use of their reading and writing ability to the betterment of self and society leaves much to be desired.

Awareness of Rights and Responsibilities

Educated people are able to know their rights and responsibilities, as well as to defend them. They are able to challenge anyone or the government if their rights are infringed. Illiterate people do not even know what their rights are, or how to defend them in the society.

Social Returns to Investment in Education

By social returns to investment in education, we mean those benefits derived by the government or the society from educating its people as a result of investment in education.

> In other words, social returns to investment in education are the benefits that a person acquires from education from which the society can benefit.

The social returns to investment in education are numerous, including the following:

Education and the Economy

Economic development is a function of education. The quest for development or modernization makes nations to invest in education. Every country endeavors to improve the standard of living of its people. This is done by improving social amenities, developing its system of communication, developing its industries, and so one. To do this, the natural resources have to be exploited for the use of the economy. No matter how large or numerous the available resources are, if the necessary skills are not available, they will remain unexploited forever. Here comes the role education plays in the economy.

Education provides employment and produces services needed by the total economy. It contributes to the GNP in the same manner as any other industry. While the economy invests in education, education, in turn, helps to improve the economy.

Education and Technology

Technological advancement is a function of education in any country. Education brings out skills and potentials of educated citizens towards modernization in any country. Education is the basis for the scientific and technological progress that is changing societies from primitive existence to modernization. Education discovers and creates talents for technological advancement of countries.

Education and Health

Education improves the health of the society. Through education, mortality rate is reduced because adequate equipment, which trained personnel can operate, is provided. Apart from this, health personnel can combat killer diseases through their exposure to education.

Education and Democracy

Education is a crucial factor in the democratic process. It increases the capacity of people to be more objective in analyzing political issues and to be more rational in judgment.

Education and Socio-Cultural Level

Education improves the socio-cultural level of a people. It eases communal tensions and promotes democratic values. It helps people to be more understanding and more accommodating. When leaders are educated on the needs and aspirations of the people, society will change for the better.

Education and Productivity

Education enhances the productivity of workers. A significant relationship exists between schooling and productivity.

Economists argue that increasing the level of education will increase the level of material output. For every additional dollar invested in education, the GNP would increase approximately by the rate of return to education.

Education and Income

The people with more education receive higher incomes than people with less education do because they produce goods that are defined as being worth more. A more equal distribution of education in the labor force tends to equalize workers' earnings distribution. This means that education determines who gets the high and low paying job in the economy. This also involves pre-tax earnings that represent the benefits accruable to society. The higher the level of education in a society, the higher the pre-tax earnings accruable to that society.

Economic Returns to Investment in Education

Education, like other sectors of a given economy, is expected to compare scarce resources on the basis of its utility to national development. In other words, financial allocation of education will depend on the rate of returns when compared to other forms of investment. In calculating economic returns to education, the following procedures must be adopted:

1. Calculating crude and adjusted social and private costs, which take care of wastage and unemployment after leaving school;
2. Adjusting for an alpha coefficient of 0.67, which takes care of unidentified variables that are likely to affect the refined cohorts of returns
3. Comparing costs and benefits to determine the profitability of investment in a given area of education;

4. Comparing the final returns obtained from the analysis using discounted cash flow technique within the rate of return formula with other forms of interest in the economy at a given point in time.

Education as an Economic Good

An economic good is a good that attracts price and that is capable of being allocated because of scarce resources. The economic system provides an arrangement for the production, exchange, and consumption of whatever is needed to satisfy human wants. In the terminology of economics, anything that satisfies a human want is a good. If a good is scarce and capable of being allocated, it is called an economic good as contrasted with a free good, such as air.

Education is an economic good regardless of whether it is produced in the public or in the private economy. Economic good is either a material or a nonmaterial good. A nonmaterial good is a service rendered to satisfy human wants. Education is a nonmaterial good, and it is a service being provided by either private or public institutions to satisfy the educational needs of individuals or communities.

Education as a Public Good

A public good is a good provided and consumed by the community for the benefits of all citizens. In other words, it is a good consumed jointly by the community or citizens.

Education is a public good in that society at large benefits from positive inputs or residual knowledge of its educated citizens. This means the consumption of education by citizens results in positive externalities (spillover effects) that benefit society at large since an educated population contributes to increased productivity in the economy.

Education as a Private Good

A private good by definition is characterized by benefits that accrue to the individual alone. Education is a private good in that individuals derived benefits from it by getting better jobs and higher lifetime earnings, by having more satisfying family lives, by adding richer cultural and civic dimensions to their existence, and by a greater sense of participation in the surrounding world.

Education as Both a Consumption and an Investment

Economists all over the world have argued that education is both a consumption and an investment.

Education as a Consumption

Consumption refers to using a good or service that gives immediate satisfaction to the person using it. Education is clearly a consumption in so far as it is desired for its own sake or in the sense that it is considered to be rewarding and intellectually stimulating in itself.

Education as a consumption can be viewed from two areas:

Education as a Leisure-Related Consumption

This refers to the leisure satisfaction one derives as a result of the level of education that he/she received. For example, an educated person may prefer listening to foreign music, which gives him more satisfaction to listening to local music as a result of his level of education. This may sound odd to an illiterate person, who may not see why such an educated person prefers listening to foreign music at his leisure time. Additionally, an educated person may enjoy visiting certain places as a result of his education, which may not be possible for an uneducated person. Education gives more personal satisfaction to educated people than to uneducated people when it comes to effective use of leisure time.

Education as a Work-related Consumption

This centers on benefits or satisfaction that educated people derive from the type of jobs they do as a result of the type of education or training they received. It is obvious that the type of job people do give them satisfaction. For example, medical doctors, lawyers, lecturers, and accountants are proud of their professions because of the satisfaction they derive from them. In this regard, education becomes a consumption.

Education as an Investment

Investment refers to the production or purchase of a good or service that gives future satisfaction.

Education is clearly an investment good in that it enables people who purchase it or participate in it to derive a future stream of benefits whether in form of income benefits from jobs they acquire by virtue of their education or in the sense that society, by providing the education, enables educated members of its labor force to add to the society's output of goods and services in the future.

The salient point here is that the type of job one gets and the benefits one derives from it at end of his training makes education an investment, and this has necessitated the huge investment in it by individuals and by the government.

Some of these benefits are the following:

- Employment opportunities;
- Higher wages or salaries (the higher the level of education, the higher the wages or salaries one receives-earning differentials);
- Develops skills and potentials inherent in person as a result of training that one is exposed to;

- Aids technological advancement consequent upon which a country is developed;
- Allows one to be conscious of and to contribute to the political situation of his environment;
- Increases social status; and
- Provides the skills needed for national development and growth.

Cardinal and Ordinal Utilities of Investment in Education

In economics generally, consumers are encouraged to choose among the available alternatives in such a way that the satisfaction derived from consuming the chosen alternative is maximized. The amount of satisfaction derived from the consumption of the chosen or best alternative by the consumer is regarded as a utility.

The information about the satisfaction derived by a consumer from various quantities of a good is contained in its utility function. Education as a consumer and as a capital good also yields utility function to its consumers or investors. Thus, in education finance, the government or investor prioritizes investment based on the utility to be derived from such investment. Utility can be measured cardinally and by rank.

Cardinal Utility of Investment in Education

When consumers buy goods or services, it is expected that such goods or services give them utility. This utility can be measured in a cardinal sense. Cardinal utility of investment in education explains clearly preferential logic in educational investment. It postulates that a consumer should determine the educational project with highest utility or satisfaction by assigning numbers representing or quantifying the amount or degree of utility associated with different educational alternatives. That is, for consumers or investors of education to have cardinal utility, they must explain why educational project A is preferred above educational project

B (or A is equal to B or less than B). This theory employs preference logic to account for different intensities of preference. For instance, if the government is faced with different educational programs such as nomadic education (A), primary education (B), technical education (C) and teachers' education (D), the cardinal approach to utility implies that the amount of utility derived from each program could be quantified as weight and presented in a preference scale. Given limited monetary and non-monetary resources at a particular period, the various educational programs could be prioritized as illustrated below:

Class	Weight		Type of Education	Position
C	50	C	Technical Education	first
B	40	B	Primary Education	second
D	20	C	Teachers Education	third
A	10	A	Nomadic Education	fourth

The reason behind the highest satisfaction derived from technical education that ranks first should be logically explained to justify the means. The differences among utility numbers could also be compared, and the comparison can lead to a statement such as "C is preferred to B twice as much as D is preferred to A."

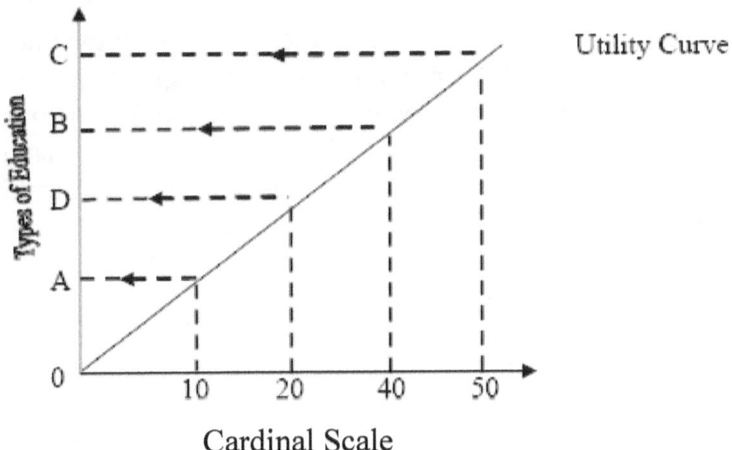

There is also what we call the marginal utility theory. This is the additional utility derived by a consumer as a result of consuming one more unit of a commodity (education). It is assumed that the additions to consumers' total utility resulting from consuming additional unit of a commodity (education) decreases as they consume more of it.

Ordinal Utility of Investment in Education

This theory was developed by the twentieth century economists led by Stutsky, Pareto, Hicks, and Allen. They postulated that utility was not measurable cardinally and that measurement was not necessary to explain consumer behavior. Ordinal utility of investment postulates that utility derived from an investment is greater or less in one situation than in another. For instance, we can say the utility derived from technical education (C) is greater than nomadic education (A) in a situation of a nation's technological development. Unlike cardinals, ordinals do not give a logical explanation as to why technical education is preferred to nomadic education. In other words, ordinal utility theory does not say anything about the intensity of preference for technical education (C) over nomadic education (A).

In ordinal utility of investment in education, educational finance stipulates that more funds should be made available to technical education than nomadic education given that higher satisfaction is derived from technical education (C) than nomadic education (A). In other words, the budget line of educational consumers or investors should favor the commodity (educational system) with a greater level of satisfaction.

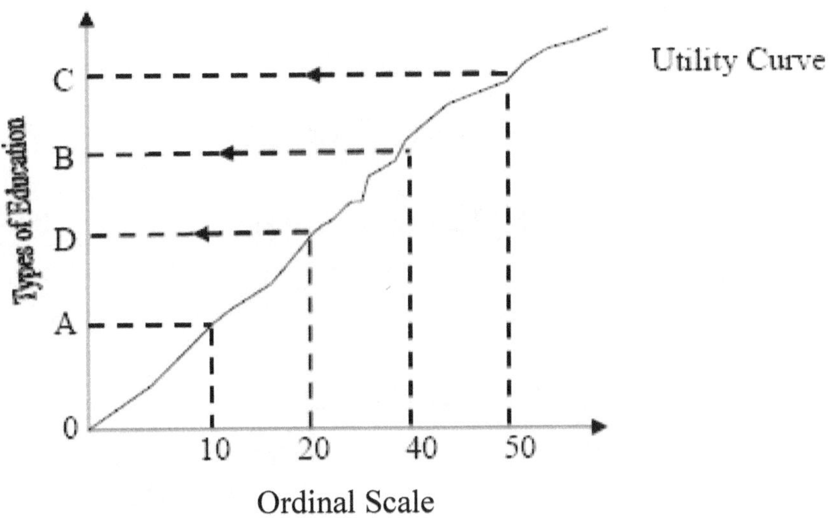
Utility Curve
C
B
D
A
0
Types of Education
10
20
40
50
Ordinal Scale

Chapter Four

The Human Capital

What is Capital?

Capital is generally regarded as a factor of production that is used up in the production of goods and services. It is but one of a number of economic factors that combine with social, political, and cultural forces in bringing the change inherent in development. Capital can be likened to a catalyst in its effects upon other factors. It is an already produced asset or good that is used as a factor input for further productive uses. Thus, in the words of Samuelson (1973), capital is regarded as an input, which is itself the output of the economy.

The word capital has different forms and can be classified as follows:

- Physical capital: physical assets such as machines, equipment, physical plants, etc.
- Human capital: Assets in form of skills and knowledge acquired by individuals
- Financial capital: Assets in form of money
- Social capital: Features of social organization such as network of individuals/households, associated norms and values that create externalities for the whole community
- Intellectual capital: cognitive skills acquired by individuals

Concept of Human Capital

Human capital has been conceptualized differently by different scholars of economics. Some look at it from the economic growth perspective, some see it as a catalyst for productivity that eventually leads to economic growth, while others look at it as the central focus or element in the production function.

Human capital refers to the stock of productive skills and technical knowledge embodied in human beings (labor) through education and training. In other words, it is regarded as the knowledge, expertise, and productive capacities that a person acquired through educational training and which enable him/her function efficiently and effectively in the society. The organization for Economic Cooperation and Development (Stroombergen and Nana 2002) posits that human capital includes the knowledge, skills, competences, and attributes embodied in individuals that facilitate the creation of personal, social, and economic well-beings.

Human capital is the stock of skills and knowledge available in a society on the basis of which modernization can take place. The formation and utilization of human capital are crucial for process of economic growth in any country. "Without growth, there can be no prosperity, hence no wealth for sharing. What is available for sharing would then be poverty. What drives growth? The simple answer is that growth is driven everywhere by productivity. The key issue about productivity is that it is brought about by human skills, human motivation, and human creativity." (Umo 1998)

A strategic investment in and utilization of human capital can place any country in a position where it will start exporting professional services and boost its foreign exchange earnings. Without this, the demand for foreign exchange will continue to grow exponentially, and such growth is unsustainable unless there is an investment in human capital formation.

The Human Capital Theory

Adam Smith (1776) was the first scholar to include human capital in his definition of capital as a capital stock of skills acquired by a nation's inhabitants, which increases wealth for the society as well as for the individuals. In 1961, 1964, and 1975, the concept of human capital was reintroduced by Nobel Laureate Theodore Schultz. It was elaborated on by Nobel Laureate Gary Becker, who is of the notion that individuals acquire skills and knowledge to increase their value in the labor market through the main mechanism of education, which in turn increases their productivity that frees resources to create new techniques and new wealth resulting in increase in economic growth.

The third authority of the human capital theory was Jacob Mincer (1962–1974), who developed the earning function that became an important empirical tool of human capital. In a nutshell, human capital theory is based on the assumptions that deliberate investments either by individuals, parents, or the society as a whole in education, training, and health lead to acquisition of knowledge, skills, and experience that make them better citizens.

However, Heitala (2003) asserts that the increase in productivity of human capital is dependent on the demand for the knowledge, skills, and abilities in the labor market and on an individual's motivation to utilize them.

The importance of the human capital theory is widely accepted by individuals and governments. For instance, the utility of the concept of human capital theory has helped to underpin a wide range of micro economic studies that help to explain decisions of individuals, households, and governments relating to education and has played a prominent role in macro-economic studies by analyzing the causes of economic growth.

Human Capital Formation/Development

Human capital occupies an important place in national development because human beings are essential factors for development. The prominence of human capital in national development accountancy is anchored on the fundamental principle that human beings are the prime movers of any development and can assist a nation to improve its GNP and the general welfare of its citizens. That means all other variables in the causal chain of development depend on it.

Human capital formation or development is sometimes referred to as manpower development. It is about imparting to people new skills, improved knowledge, and constructive changes in their behaviors. It is regarded as the process of acquiring and increasing the number of people who have the skills and experience that are crucial for the economic and political development of a country through education and training. In other words, it is regarded as the process of increasing knowledge, skills, and capabilities of people in a country for productive uses.

Human capital development is of great importance to the individuals and the society because of the new challenges in the total environment especially in this era of globalization where the economic response to the introduction of new technologies and products is paramount.

In Africa, Mureith and Wasikama (2000) observe that the level of human resource development is low with its primary enrollment far from universal, characterized by gender disparity and declining maintenance. This poses a future challenge to the continent. Meanwhile, in Nigeria, Aigbokhan, Imahe, and Ailemen (2007) discovered that insufficient and uncertain budgetary allocations to the education sub-sector resulted in the deterioration of the impact of educational expenditure on human capital development.

Human capital could be formed or developed through investment in formal education at all levels, implementation of on-the-job training, seminars, and workshops, through experiences, and interaction with other individuals sharing ideas. For any meaningful human capital development policy to take place, the following parameters must among others be taken into consideration:

- Identification of the principal critical manpower shortages in each sector of the economy. This means that most critical manpower shortages in all the sectors in the economy must be identified and analyzed (e.g., banking sector, educational sector, industrial sector, public sector, agricultural sector, and so on).
- Identification of surpluses of trained and unskilled manpower, and the reasons for such surpluses.
- The program of action for human resource development based on logical expectation of growth in the economy must be set and implemented.
- The rate of modernization of a given country must also be taken into consideration. This means, meaningful human resource development must take note of the rate of modernization in all sectors of the economy.
- The mix of human resources among low, middle, and top levels as well as among different skills to guide against manpower glut and shortages in certain critical areas of the economy must also be taken into consideration.

Investments in Human Capital

Human capital investment is an indispensable component of development process. Generally, investments in human capital like other investments are current costs (both direct and indirect) incurred with the expectation that these costs will yield stream of benefits (economic and noneconomic) over a period of time in the future. Usually, the decision to invest in human capital either by individuals, parents, or the society is a function of the expected returns in terms of increased individuals' learning capacity, employment prospects, income distribution, or a firm's or an organization's productivity and economic growth. However, the major determinants of investment decisions in human capital are acquisition cost and expected rate of return.

Acquisition cost relates to the cost of acquiring human capital and this affects investment decisions of individuals, government, and the society at large. The expected rate of return depends on whether the benefits exceed the cost.

Impact of Human Capital on Economic Growth

Investment in human capital directly impacts growth and the productivity capacity of any economy. The human capital investment has both micro and macro evidences which account for differences in growth rate across countries. This growth rate is reflected in each countries' (GDP).

Table 1: GDP Per Capita (%) in some African Countries

Countries	1975–1984	1995–2004
Benin	1.1	1.5
Burkina Faso	1.0	1.6
Chad	-2.4	8.9
Ghana	-2.8	2.1
Mauritania	-0.7	0.6
Morocco	2.0	2.4
Nigeria	-3.4	2.5
Senegal	-0.7	1.9
South Africa	0.0	1.6
Tunisia	2.6	3.8
Zimbabwe	-1.1	-3.5

Source: Population Reference Bureau's 2007 Data Sheet

Table 2: GDP Per Capita (%) in some Asian Countries

Countries	1975–1984	1995–2004
Georgia	4.6	6.6
India	1.8	4.1
Iran	-2.9	2.9
Nepal	1.2	1.4
Saudi Arabia	-5.1	0.3
Sri Lanka	3.6	3.8
United Arab Emirates	-3.2	0.5
Viet Nam	-	5.5
Yemen	-	0.7

Source: Population Reference Bureau's 2007 data sheet.

Mechanism of Human Capital Impacts on Economic Growth

Sexton and Hall (2000) identify two mechanisms through which human capital could influence economic growth. They are the following:

1. creation of new knowledge commonly referred to as Schumpeterian growth. This is the growth attributable to increases in human capital (innovation and entrepreneurial aspects included). It is believed that the number of educated individuals (in the form of scientists, technicians, investors, and similar professions) in a particular society affects the technological prospects of the economy through the development of new processes and technologies.
2. diffusion and transmission of knowledge acquired in the process of education that enables individuals to understand, digest and transform new information to enhance better use of new technologies leading to inventions and innovations.

It is the human capital that accounts for a significant proportion of residual of economic growth that cannot be explained.

Predictors of Human Capital Flight

Human capital flight refers to brain drain from one country to another. There has been a serious brain drain from developing countries to industrialized countries. Owen (Appleton and Teal 1998), reporting the extent of the flight of the most educated Africans from the continent in 1993 emphasized that, in the UK, there were 134, 500 Africans: 14,500 had bachelor's degrees and 4,600 had advanced degrees. Of all the ethnic minorities in the United Kingdom, Africans formed the largest percentage with recognized educational qualifications.

Williams (Appleton and Teal, 1998) also pointed out that as of 1994, an estimated 100,000 skilled Africans worked in Europe and North America. These skilled Africans were typically doctors, research scientists, and university teachers. The emigration of many highly educated Africans has posed a serious problem to the economies of most African countries in the continent as this leads to scarcity of prime movers of economic development in these countries, although governments incurred the social costs of higher education, the emigration of graduates means that their countries do not benefit from the investments in education.

The factors responsible for human capital flight are the following:

- **High Level of Unemployment Rate**

The purpose of education in any country is to make citizens become useful to themselves and the society at large. This goal is defeated where there is a high level of unemployment. No educated person, no matter how skilled, can be regarded as a human capital unless he/she turns his/her skill, knowledge, and expertise acquired through education into productive uses for his/her own benefit and the benefit of the society. Many restive graduates roam about the streets of the developing countries, especially in Nigeria, because of the problem of unemployment. Many highly skilled Nigerians are found in Europe and America working and contributing immensely to the growth of GDP of these countries.

- **Political Instability**

No rational highly skilled labor will be willing to be wasted where there are incessant political crises. A War Zone area depletes itself of human capital and this will have a negative effect on its development. Political instability encourages brain drain and hence, serious economic problems.

- **Employers' Unwillingness to Pay Wages Commensurate with the Level of Skills**

'Employers' unwillingness to pay a rate commensurate with level of skills acquired by their employees encourages human capital flight in that many highly skilled professions are often underpaid in the developing countries. These underpaid professionals look elsewhere for higher rates and hence, brain drain.

- **Lack of Environmental Conduciveness**

By lack of environmental conduciveness, we mean those environmental factors that affect the efficiency of workers negatively. The environmental factors such as harsh weather, incessant blackouts (irregular supply of electricity), and emission and disposal of hazardous chemicals and waste products into the environments. These factors cripple the potency of highly skilled laborers, as they will not be able to operate efficiently and productively in these conditions.

Regular blackouts in Nigeria, for example, do not encourage research, new innovations, nor technologies upon which human capital could embark for development. Compared to much physical capital, human capital is long-lived and more irreversible; if people are not given adequate care in term of environmental conduciveness in the country, this will have consequences on their productivity and can lead to human capital flight.

Manpower Planning Strategies

Manpower is conceptualized as people who possess education and training required to fill occupations and posts considered critical for socio-economic development and growth of the country concerned (Harbison and Myean 1964). Manpower planning, therefore, is a process through which human resources meant for the development and growth in a particular country or firm are acquired, utilized, improved, and preserved.

The following strategies can be adopted for manpower planning:

- **The Economic Strategy**

This is a strategy based on the assumption that manpower forecasting must be related to wage structure as well as to training. It also suggests that most functional organizations must relate their manpower planning to happenings in the economy because of the symbiotic relationship between human capital development and aggregate output in the economy.

- **The Technical Strategy**

It is an approach that prescribes that skill requirements by any organization in a country would be determined by technological developments in the various terrains of the economy rather than through market process. To do otherwise is to invest in irrelevant human infrastructure that will not contribute to both the technical and economic efficiencies of a functional organization or society.

- **Ratio of Saturation Method**

This method or technique is based on the assessment of manpower requirement by the degree of saturation of the total stock of labor with high-level skills. It relates high-level manpower to the total employed labor force (per 1,000 workers). It is widely used by capital-intensive organizations like energy and automobile industries. Its main emphases are

1. to calculate the level of high-level manpower to the total labor force for a number of years in the past.
2. to assess the total stock of labor force for the period covered by a plan period.
3. to project the requirements for high-level manpower by extrapolation of past trends. Its major advantage is that it allows for the replacement of saturated high-level manpower in a given system or organization.

- **The Staff Normative Strategy**

It is a more precise method because it takes into account the main factors affecting the magnitude of manpower requirements. It is concerned with the drawing up of labor balances for the effective and efficient running of a firm or organization. Such balances would take into account the needs of all divisions by skills or professions.

Manpower Auditing

It is a process whereby an organization or a firm assesses the shortages or surpluses available to the organization or firm by manpower categories. It is also known as manpower stocktaking. The main objectives of manpower auditing are

- to identify the areas of wastage with a view to mapping out appropriate strategies for rectifying the situation.

- to ensure rational manpower distribution in a firm or organization.
- to identify replacement, expansion requirements and substitution between different levels of workers and productivity changes.

Chapter Five

Costs Of Education

What is Cost?

Babalola (1992) defines cost as a measure of what is given up in order to produce or consume a commodity. In general, the concept of cost comes into play in the production of goods or services. Cost can be expressed in terms of money or in non-monetary terms. Cost is regarded as the effort and sacrifice needed to produce goods and services. Longe (1987) stresses that real cost corresponds to opportunity cost which holds that the cost of a good shall be measured in terms of the unproduced goods that could have been produced with the input used to produce the goods in question. In the economic life of any good, it is assumed that there is always a choice of alternatives. That is, the cost of any choice must be expressed in terms of the opportunity forgone to achieve the alternative. Cost also refers to the resources that are used in the production of capital assets.

What is Educational Cost?

Babalola (1992), in his definition, refers to educational cost as a measure of what a student, an institution of learning or the public has to give up in order to educate an individual or a group of people.

Adedeji (2002) defines educational cost as the monetary and non-monetary values used up in the process of educating an individual or a group of individuals.

Madumere (1989), stressing what educational cost means, says it refers to real resources that are used up in the production of human capital (i.e., educated students).

Educational cost comprises all the inputs (physical and human resources) that are used up in producing educated students. These inputs (resources) are measured and expressed in monetary terms and include not only the cost to the individuals and government agencies directly associated with the development and operation of a project, but all of the costs that have to be incurred to produce the intended benefits of the projects (Madumere 1989).

Educational cost, therefore, refers to the real resources used and those resources forgone in the process of producing human capital. That is, it comprises both direct and indirect costs incurred in educating an individuals or a group of individuals.

Types of Cost in Education

Education incurs many types of costs, as discussed below:

Direct Cost

This refers to the cost that is directly linked to educational activity. Direct cost also refers to the expenditure on educational inputs that are incurred by government and individuals (students).

According to Babalola (2002), it is the value of items directly purchased by the educational system. Direct cost of education includes school fees, expenditures of books and uniforms for students, transport fares, teachers' salaries, and furniture for students and staff of the system.

Indirect Cost

Indirect cost refers to what individuals and the society lose in order to acquire education. It is the opportunity cost in terms of earnings forgone for acquisition of education. While a student is continuing his education, he deprives the labor market of his services and deprives himself of certain income. These services and income forgone by the student are regarded as opportunity costs.

Indirect cost also refers to the cost, which cannot be directly linked with the production of educational products and services.

Opportunity Cost

Opportunity cost is the cost of alternatives forgone. In other words, opportunity cost of education represents the value of the real sacrifices that have to be incurred in the process of educating an individual or a group of individuals. It means sacrificing the opportunity to spend these same resources on something else.

Money Cost

The money cost of education is the amount of money that is directly spent on educational resources (inputs) as a result of educating people. Money cost can be subdivided into capital and current expenditures.

Institutional Cost

This can be divided into two categories, namely capital cost and recurrent cost. Capital cost comprises the cost of durable educational inputs such as land, school buildings, furniture, equipment, water, electricity, school vehicles, audio-visual aids, and other unspecified costs. Most capital stock except land depreciates in value overtime. This depreciation is taken care of in the valuation process, a given percentage of the value (the present cost of replacing the stock) less depreciation. Another process of stock evaluation is by estimating its market value given the current information to facilitate such estimation.

A huge amount of money is usually involved in capital costs, and this normally raises special financial problems. In other words, if capital is borrowed, it must be repaid with accrued interest.

Recurrent cost comprises the institutional expenditure on items such as teachers' and non-teachers' salaries and fringe benefits, consumable goods such as stationery, materials cost, repairs and maintenance costs, and utility bills. These costs occur yearly in the budget and hence are referred to as recurrent costs. Institutional costs of education, therefore, refer to the costs borne by educational institutions.

Social Cost of Education

Social cost refers to the costs borne by the public through government. According to Babalola (1992), they are costs borne by the public through the government's expenditures on additional living costs, on students, books, uniforms, transportation, furniture, equipment, buildings, salaries, and other consumables by the institutions. They are also earnings forgone (before taxes) as a result of withdrawing the services of children from the labor market. He went further to say that they are simply the addition of private and institutional costs of education minus tuition and scholarship.

Okedara (1979) defines social cost as the institutional cost (scholarship included) minus tuition cost plus private cost, tuition included minus scholarship.

When the government provides tuition and textbooks to students, they are said to be added to the social cost rather than the private cost.

Private Cost of Education

Private cost refers to the cost borne by the parents, guardians, and individuals. They are the monetary value of all what individuals, households, families, or private institutions invest in education. Private cost consists of both direct and indirect costs. Private direct cost includes tuition fees, pocket money, transportation costs, books and uniforms, and accommodations. The private indirect cost, on the other hand, includes the earnings forgone by a student at a different level during the period of education while his counterparts are engaged in productive sectors of the economy and are earning incomes.

Capital Cost of Education

Capital cost represents the costs of durable items such as land, building, machine, equipment, and the cost of maintaining them. Capital costs relate to more durable items (land, buildings, and equipment) that render useful service over a period of years if properly maintained; hence, major repairs and maintenance are also capital costs since they prolong the useful life of capital items.

Recurrent / Current Cost of Education

Recurrent cost is the recurrent expenditure of the educational system including salaries and wages paid to teaching and non-teaching staff as well as the cost of consumables. Current cost can also be referred to as operating cost. Current cost, by and large, relates to personnel services and consumable supplies that are used up within one fiscal year and must therefore be renewed regularly.

Efficiency Cost of Education

Efficiency cost is the cost incurred when output is increased with minimum inputs. Efficiency cost, in other words, is the cost incurred when minimal educational inputs are used to achieve the set goals or to increase educational output (learning results) without an equivalent increase in its costs.

Factor Cost of Education

This refers to the prices paid for factors of production such as teachers, equipments, buildings, and materials. Factor cost may be tied to quality and standard.

Patent Cost

Patent cost refers to the costs of preparing disclosures, reports, and other documents required by educational institutions.

Transportation Cost of Education

Transportation cost refers to the costs incurred for freight, express, cartage, postage, and other transportation services relating either to goods and services purchased or delivered by educational institutions, government, or individuals in the process of acquiring education.

Incremental Cost of Education

Incremental cost is synonymous with marginal cost. Incremental cost refers to the additional cost to the total cost of education as a result of one unit change in educational outputs or change in the level or nature of an educational activity.

Sunk Cost of Education

Sunk cost is a fixed expenditure that is borne or to be borne as a result of a past mistake in respect of a contractual agreement with other entities (Babalola 1992). Sunk cost is the irrelevant cost of education..

Explicit and Implicit Costs of Education

Explicit cost of education is the actual amount paid in educational transaction. It is usually reflected in accounting statement.

Implicit cost of education, on the other hand, is the value of opportunities being forgone in order to acquire education. In this case, no actual cash payment is involved (Babalola, 1992).

Marginal Cost of Education

This is the change in the total cost as a result of one unit change in the level of educational output. For example, marginal cost of training one more student apart from the total number of students trained initially per session would be costs of equipment, teachers, non-teaching staff, goods, and services per that additional student. Marginal cost, therefore, refers to the cost of education that results from increasing total output by one more unit output. Marginal cost can be expressed as follows:

$$\text{Marginal Cost} = \frac{\text{Change in Total Cost}}{\text{Change in Output}}$$

$$MC = \frac{\Delta TC}{\Delta Q}$$

Effectiveness Cost

This is the cost per unit of educational output. In other words, effectiveness cost is the cost per unit of achievement in an educational system.

Total Cost of Education

This refers to the whole money expended on education by an individual or government or institution. Total cost is the sum of either indirect and direct costs, fixed and variable costs, or capital and current costs depending on the circumstantial issues on ground.

Total cost could be expressed as follows:

$$\text{Total Cost} = \text{Indirect Cost} + \text{Direct Cost}$$
$$TC = IC + DC$$

$$\text{Total Cost} = \text{Fixed Cost} + \text{Variable Cost}$$
$$TC = FC + VC$$

$$\text{Total Cost} = \text{Recurrent Cost} + \text{Capital Cost}$$
$$TC = RC + CC$$

Variable Cost and Fixed Cost

Variable cost is the cost incurred, which varies or changes with the size of an educational activity. Variable cost occurs when there is an expansion in educational activities. For example, the costs of stationery and student services are variable costs because when enrollment is increased, these costs will definitely increase with this increased enrollment.

Fixed cost is the cost incurred whether or not there is an operation of educational activity. In other words, fixed cost remains fixed whether or not there are teaching, learning, and other educational activities (Babalola, 1992). Examples of fixed cost are rents, rates, and insurance.

Unit Cost of Education

Unit cost of education is the average of a total cost in education. The unit cost is the ratio of the total cost of an item to the total number of characteristics being determined. Unit Cost can be expressed as follows:

$$\text{Unit Cost} = \frac{\text{Total Cost}}{\text{Output}}$$

$$\text{Unit Cost} = \frac{TC}{Q}$$

Some of the unit costs in education are expressed below:

$$\text{Teacher's Cost:} \quad \frac{\text{Total teachers' salaries and allowances}}{\text{Total number of teachers}}$$

This teacher cost can be subdivided into graduate teachers cost and non-graduate teachers' cost.

$$\text{Graduate Teacher's Cost:} \quad \frac{\text{Total graduate teachers' salaries and allowances}}{\text{Total number of graduate teachers}}$$

Non-graduate
teacher's cost: $\frac{\text{Total non-graduate teachers' salaries \& allowances}}{\text{Total number of non-graduate teachers}}$

Non
Teacher's Cost: $\frac{\text{Total non teaching staff salaries and allowances}}{\text{Total number of non teaching staff}}$

Cost per class: $\frac{\text{Total school expenditure}}{\text{Number of classes}}$

Cost per teaching hour: $\frac{\text{Total school expenditure}}{\text{The number of teaching hours}}$

Equipment Cost Per Student: $\frac{\text{Total school expenditure on equipment}}{\text{Total student population.}}$

Books and Stationary Cost Per Student: $\frac{\text{Expenditure on books and stationary}}{\text{Total school enrollment}}$

Cost per stream: $\frac{\text{Total school expenditure}}{\text{The number of streams}}$

Average Cost per student: $\frac{\text{Total school expenditure}}{\text{Total school enrollment}}$

Recurrent Cost per student: $\frac{\text{Total school recurrent expenditure}}{\text{Total student population}}$

Capital cost per student: $\frac{\text{Total School capital expenditure}}{\text{Total student population.}}$

Cost Analysis in Education

The on-going global financial meltdown has profoundly altered the financial posture of educational systems everywhere. With most countries' educational budgets - frozen or shrinking, the daunting question is where to make the cuts? In addition, several other critical educational issues presently plague both developed and developing nations. These issues include the following:

- The erosion of educational quality and relevance;
- The increasing numbers of educated unemployed and the growing incongruity between the world of education and the world of work; and
- the gross educational inequalities that penalize females, the poor, and various ethnic minority groups.

Given these critical educational issues, the central challenge to educational managers everywhere is to find ways to use their limited resources more efficiently and effectively. Cost analysis, therefore, is a versatile and potentially tool in the hands of educational managers to meet this challenge.

Calculation of Unit Costs in Education

Example 1

The expenditures of a primary school with a student population of 1,230, a teacher-pupil ratio of 1:30 and $30,000 for the salaries and allowances of the non-teaching staff for the 2007 is presented in the table below:

Item	Item Descriptions	Actual Expenditure
1	Staff salaries and allowances	$240,000
2	Purchase of school van	$58,000
3	Administrative and office expenses	$8,500
4	Transport and traveling	$9,500
5	Computer Equipment	$7,500

Item	Item Descriptions	Actual Expenditure
6	Maintenance of Equipment & Furniture	$1,800
7	Construction of Modern Toilets	$115,000
8	School Board Expenses	$4,000
9	Utility Bills	$15,000
10	Insurance	$3,200

Exercises

1. Find the unit capital cost of education in this school for the year 2007.
2. What percentage of the capital expenditure was spent on computer equipment?
3. Find the recurrent cost per student.
5. Determine the unit cost of education in this school for the year 2007.
6. Calculate the average salary cost per teacher.

Solutions

1. Items of Capital Cost

Purchase of school van	58,000
Computer equipment	7,500
Construction of Modern Lavatory +	115,000
Total capital cost	$180,500

$$\text{Unit capital cost} = \frac{\text{Total Capital cost}}{\text{Student population}}$$

$$= \frac{\$180{,}500}{1230}$$

$$= \$146.75$$

2. The percentage of capital expenditure spent on computer equipment

Capital expenditure = $180,500
Computer equipment = $7,500

$$\frac{\text{Computer equipment cost}}{\text{Capital expenditure}} \times 100$$

$$= \frac{\$7{,}500}{\$180{,}500} \times \frac{100}{1}$$

= 4.16%

3. Items of Recurrent Cost

Staff salaries and allowances	240,000
Administrative and office expenses	8,500
Transportation and traveling	9,500
Maintenance of equipment and furniture	1,800
School board expenses	4,000
Utility bills	15,000
Insurance	+ 3,200
Total Recurrent Cost	$282,000

$$\text{Recurrent Cost per student} = \frac{\text{Total recurrent cost}}{\text{Student population}}$$

$$= \frac{\$282{,}000}{1230}$$

= $229.27

4. Total cost of education

Total capital cost		180,500
Total recurrent cost	+	282,000
Total cost of education		$462,500

$$\text{Unit cost of education} = \frac{\text{Total Cost of education}}{\text{Student population}}$$

$$= \frac{\$462,500}{1230}$$

$$= \$376.02$$

5. The average salary of cost per teacher

Total staff salaries and allowances		240,000
Less non-teaching staff salaries and allowances	-	30,000
Teaching staff salaries and allowances		$210,000

Teacher-pupil ratio 1:30

$$\text{Number of teachers} = \frac{1230}{30} \quad \frac{\text{Student population}}{\text{Number of pupils}}$$

$$= \text{41 teachers per teacher}$$

$$\text{Average salary cost per teacher} = \frac{\$210,000}{41} = \$5,121.95$$

Example 2

A government junior college has a student population of 2,040 with total staff strength of thirty-nine on an average monthly emolument of $17,500. The expenditures for the 2008 academic year ended as follows:

Procurement of a school bus	$700,000
Stationeries and other consumable plants	$64,000
Sinking of a borehole	$80,000
Utility bills	$18,000/month
Maintenance and fueling of school bus	$20,000/month
Inter-house sports competition	$57,000
Two computer sets	$90,000
Speech and prize giving day ceremony	$48,000
Purchase of photocopier	$120,000
Laboratory chemicals	$21,000
Construction of four additional classrooms	$650,000/each
Grading/clearing of field for visitors' parking	$75,000
Laboratory equipment	$40,000
Term imprest	$15,000

Exercises

1. What is the recurrent cost per student for the year?
2. Calculate the capital cost per student for the year.
3. Determine the average salary cost.
4. What percentage of the capital expenditure was spent on procurement of a school bus?

Solutions

An academic year comprises nine months		This is the academic calendar year
Total staff emoluments per month 39 x $17,500	=	$682,500
Total staff emoluments for twelve months	=	$8,190,000

Utility bills per month	$18,000
Utility bills for twelve months	$216,000
Maintenance and fuelling of school bus per month	$20,000
Maintenance and fueling of school bus for nine months	$180,000

Term imprest $15,000. A term is three months long.
Three months x $15,000 = $45,000

Construction of four additional classrooms at
$650,000 each.4 x $650,000 = $2,600,000

1. Total Recurrent Cost

Total staff emoluments for twelve months	$8,190,000
Stationeries and other consumable plants	$64,000
Utility bills for twelve months	$216,000
Maintenance & fueling of school bus for nine months	$180,000
Inter-house sports competition	$57,000
Speech and prize giving day ceremony	$48,000
Laboratory chemicals	$21,000
Grading/clearing of field for visitors' parking lot	$75,000
Total imprest	$45,000
Total recurrent costs	$8,896,000

$$\text{Recurrent cost per student} = \frac{\text{Total Recurrent cost}}{\text{Student population}}$$

$$= \frac{\$8.896.000}{2040}$$

$$= \$4,360.78$$

2. Total Capital Cost

Procurement of a school	$700,000
Sinking of a borehole	$80,000
Two computer sets	$90,000
Purchase of photocopier	$120,000
Construction of four additional classrooms at $650,000 each	$2,600,000
Laboratory equipment	$40,000
Total Capital Cost	$3,630,000

$$\text{Capital cost per student} = \frac{\text{Total Capital Cost}}{\text{Student Population}}$$

$$= \frac{\$3,630,000}{2040}$$

$$= \$1,779.41$$

3. The Average Salary Cost

Total salary emoluments	$8,190,000
Staff strength	39

$$\text{Average salary cost} = \frac{\$8,190,000}{39}$$

Average salary cost for twelve months $210,500

4. The percentage of the capital expenditure spent on procurement of a school bus:

Total capital expenditure	$3,630,000
Procurement of a school	$700,000

$$\frac{\$700,000}{\$3,630,000} \times \frac{100}{1} = 19.28\%$$

Uses of Cost Analysis

Cost analysis reveals what is being given up in terms of other alternatives for which a given set of resources might be used. In this case, it is an essential element in internal decision making since a decision or choice from among alternatives means giving up certain options.

Cost analysis can uncover serious internal wastages and inefficiency and possible ways to eliminate them. It can also suggest ways to enhance the external productivity of education and the benefits accruing to individuals and society from well-directed investments in education.

Cost analysis is an essential tool for testing the economic feasibility of broad national education plans, of specific project plans, and of proposed innovations.

The careful analysis of cost provides a means of control over the internal operation of educational systems. Such a control is necessary to ensure wise and proper use of funds.

Finally, cost analysis provides a means for examining educational managers on which ways resources are used. The analysis may give evidence concerning the rationality of the organization.

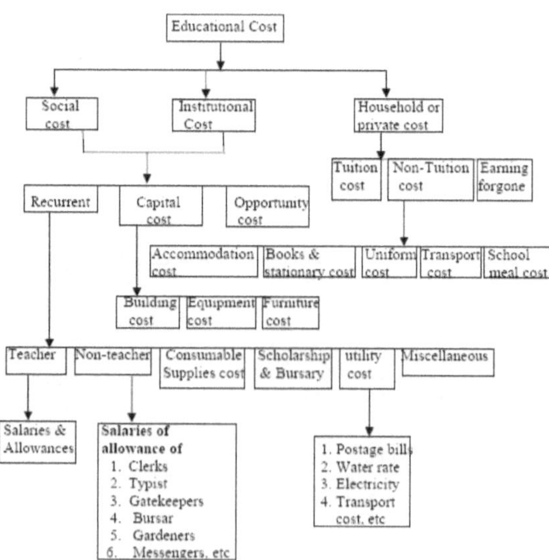

Cost Escalation in Education Industry

The cost of education has been rising since the last three decades. This cost has been escalating at an alarming rate, and the following factors are responsible for it:

Increased Demand for Education

There is an upsurge of demand for education. This is due to importance attached to the acquisition of education and also due to population explosion. In order to accommodate and satisfy this demand, governments of the world have to spend more money to provide facilities in terms of men and materials.

Apart from government spending, increased demand has also spurred cost incurred by private individuals. Since the government can no longer bear the burden alone, education cost sharing formula is being adopted between the government and individuals. It is not surprising that private individuals pay more than government these days.

Educational Wastages

Wastages in education refer to repeats, failures, and dropouts. Increases in the number of dropouts and repeaters result in much higher costs and a heavy waste of scarce educational resources. This means that the government will have to budget additional money to care for repeaters in the next academic year.

Geographical Distribution of Schools

The geographical distribution of schools and their administrative offices such as Local Education Districts (LEDs) in all local government areas make the government spend more money. For example, Lagos State Government in Nigeria has LEDs and schools in all the local government areas of the state, and those offices and schools have to be funded and maintained. If these offices are combined under one roof, the government could spend less.

Changes in the Salary Structure of Personnel

Upward review of the salaries and allowances of personnel in the education industry gears up the cost of education. Education industry seems to be the largest industry that has many personnel in terms of teaching and non-teaching staff. Because this industry has its schools everywhere, governments and private owners have to employ and spend more on the personnel in terms of salaries and allowances annually.

Under-Utilization of Educational Facilities, Equipment, and Personnel

The unit cost per student is substantially influenced by the rate of utilization of personnel, educational facilities, and equipment. Many studies have shown that most of our resources are underutilized and being wasted. This is evident in our institutions of learning where expensive buildings and equipment often stand idle much of the time. If these resources are fully utilized—especially during holidays for seminars, workshops, and conferences—they should have generated funds for the institutions. Yet, under-utilization does not reduce depreciation on such facilities. All these increase the costs of education to the government.

Drive for technology

The cost of education will continue to rise as long as technology is emphasized. The manpower needed to man the instruments has to be adequately trained so that the equipment can be properly handled. In a bid to advance technology, machines and educational equipment as well as teaching aids must be procured, thus escalating the costs of education.

Influence of Government Policies and International Development Policies

Government policies such as free education for all and universal basic education make the government spend too much money on education. This is because every facility has to be provided and funded by the government in order to fulfill these policies. Now that there is a millennium development goal in education, this requires huge capital outlays for its actualization.

Capital Project Investments

The issue of capital projects such as construction of classrooms, library, introduction technology workshop, and laboratories is one of the factors responsible for cost escalation in the education industry. The reason is that these projects have to be constructed or provided in various areas where schools are built or sited.

Political Instability

The unstable political climate is at times responsible for government closure of schools for a period only to resume later for continuation of the session. During the period of closure, government pays the personnel and maintains the facilities, and by the time the schools are reopened, government has to pay the staff again. All these increase cost of education.

Remedies for Cost Escalation in the Education Industry

Foreign Assistance

Foreign assistance could be sought from developed countries and international bodies like United States Agency for International

Development (USAID), United Nations Educational, Scientific and Cultural Organization (UNESCO) and similar agencies. This assistance could come in the form of human, financial, and material resources. International bodies or developed countries can send specialists to teach in some of our schools; they can assist by funding researches. They can also send materials such as textbooks and teaching aids. All these reduce costs of education in developing countries.

Education Tax and Endowment Fund

Private organizations should be made to pay education taxes, and the proceeds from this could be used to finance education. Individuals can also be made to be involved in an education endowment fund to finance education.

In Nigeria, for example, 2 percent of each company's gross profit is being paid to the Education Trust Fund (ETF) annually to finance education. Through this, remarkable changes have taken place in our educational system in terms of buildings, facilities, and equipment.

Educational Consultancy Services

Educational Institutions should be involved in consultancy services to generate funds for themselves.

Alumni and Parent-Teacher Association (PTA) Involvement

The PTA can assist in funding through construction of more classrooms, supplies to the school libraries, and other ways. Alumni associations should also invest in their institutions. For example, alumni fees being collected from graduating students in higher institutions should be used to finance some of the capital projects in the parent institutions.

Use of Local Materials

Educational institutions should make use of local materials instead of importing them.

Teachers and students should be encouraged to patronize local teaching aid stores, equipment and facilities for teaching, and the learning process in the schools. These help to bring the costs of education to a minimum level in the country.

Rationalization of Courses

Government should also rationalize courses in our educational system with a view to avoiding duplication of institutions of the same status in many locations in the country.

Establishment of Counseling Units

Counseling Units should be provided in our educational system to help in the identification of potentials inherent in students, as a result of which they would be placed in the proper areas or fields of specialization. This will help in reducing educational wastages.

Textbook and Stationery Requirement Policy

There should be a policy to reduce textbook requirements by schools. In a situation where schools recommend an average of three books per subject, there should be only one basic required textbook. Furthermore, governments should take the responsibility of mandating the State Library Board to open branches to serve students in all local government areas and each branch should run a bookshop where students can buy books at lower costs than the commercial rates offered at other shops in the town. Otherwise, governments should put in place price control mechanisms to regulate the prices of books and stationary in developing countries.

Rising Cost of Education and the Principle of Fiscal Justice

The principle of fiscal justice, otherwise known as the principle of prime beneficiary, is a concept emphasized by Samuel (2003) to explain why cost of education is rising at all levels in Nigeria. The principle implies that whoever carries the largest benefits of education should bear its largest cost. Reiterating this, Samuel (2003) states that, "The strategy prescribes that he who takes the lion share of the benefits of education must bear the biggest cost. In essence, if parents and their wards or government reap more benefits from education, the cost and financing of education should tilt heavily towards them" (42).

This principle explains why the cost allocation mechanism in education industry has changed over time. From all indications, the private cost of education is escalating at all levels every year. It is assumed that individuals receive greater benefits of education than what is obtainable to the government, and the government is drifting away from more sharing of the cost burden in education.

In a study carried out by Akinyemi (2005) on the analysis of unit costs of public primary education in Lagos State of Nigeria, it was found that though both the private and social costs per pupil escalated every year, the household spending (private cost) per child was higher than what the government was spending (social cost) in the periods under study. While households were incurring more than 70 percent of the total cost per child, the government was incurring less than 30 percent of the same cost per child. In Kenya, a survey carried out by Mitha, et al (1995) on parents' contribution to primary schools indicated that households met about 95 percent of school recurrent expenditure in the forms of textbooks, stationery, furniture, school uniforms, examination fees, transportation, and school meals. A similar study carried out by Samuel (2003) for the World Bank on public expenditure in Lagos State of Nigeria, discovered that the household unit cost for primary education was ₦33,000 (US $235.70) while the average public unit cost was under ₦3,000 (US $21.43) for the same level. In secondary education, according to him, households paid ₦42,000 (US $300) per student while the average public unit cost was less than ₦3,000 (US $7.14).

Borthwick (1999), studying the private and public expenditure on secondary education in Australia in 1997, found that the level of private expenditure, which originated from individuals and enterprises, was more than what the government expended (public expenditure). He estimated the private expenditure to be $4.4 billion (55 percent) while 45 percent of all training expenditure was incurred by the Australian government.

In a similar study of public and private investment in education in Kenya conducted by Abagi (2002), it was discovered that a household spent Kshs 43,950, (Kenyan shillings) and Kshs 4,620 annually on one child enrolled in an urban primary school and a rural primary school respectively while the government spent Kshs 2,774 per primary school child.

The researches highlighted above reveal that the principle of fiscal justice has been put in place in cost allocation mechanism in education and that it is the households that bear the greater cost of education consequent to the greater benefits received.

The Benefiter-Pays Principle

The benefiter-pays principle is synonymous with the principle of fiscal justice. It has its origin in the polluters-pay principle, now broadly referred to as the user-pays principle.

The benefiter-pays principle implies that those who benefit from something should contribute, and those who don't benefit should not have to pay. The principle is supported by the underlying philosophical concept of justice and fairness that argues that it is unjust and inequitable to pass debts incurred on education now to the next generation while the current generation enjoys the benefits of this educational investment.

Hence, it advocates that the present benefiters should pay for what they have taken or gained.

The Principle of Fiscal Sustainability

The principle of fiscal sustainability explains the evil of intergenerational equity and deferred tax burdens. It proffers that government should be able to manage its finances in such a way that it can meet its spending commitments, both now and in the future.

The principle of fiscal sustainability postulates that the present generation should not impose budgetary burdens on future generations. They should not leave behind deficits and debts that future people are obliged to pay, and should ensure, as much as possible, that future people will be able to enjoy a reasonable standard of life. The fiscal sustainability principle ensures that future generations of taxpayers do not end up paying for social resources and services that the current generation benefits from but does not pay for. In other words, it emphasizes that future generations of taxpayers do not face an unmanageable bill for government services provided to the current generation.

By implication, the principle requires the maintenance of appropriate economic, social, and environmental conditions through time to ensure that the well-being of future generations is not compromised by the activities of the current generation. On this note, leaving a higher tax burden for the next generation would amount to compromising their wellbeing, presumably because future individuals would have less disposable income to enhance it. This does not contribute to the sustaining of wellbeing into the next generation.

In education, future students of our educational institutions should not be made to pay for educational resources and services that the current students enjoy now but do not pay for. Current students should be rather made to pay for whatever resources or services being enjoyed by them now.

Cost Efficiency and Cost Effectiveness in Education

Cost efficiency and cost effectiveness are often taken to mean the same thing. There is a clear distinction between cost efficiency and cost effectiveness.

Cost Efficiency

Efficiency, by definition, means the ability to produce or achieve a desired result or goal with a minimum effort, expense or minimum application of resource inputs. Cost efficiency, therefore, implies that a set goal or a desired result is achieved and the cost incurred is minimized. Relating it to education, cost efficiency refers to minimization of educational input costs for desired educational benefits/outcomes.

Cost Effectiveness

Effectiveness refers to adopting the cheapest way through which the goals set would be attained. Cost effectiveness, therefore, implies the application of the most efficient way of achieving the desired results/objectives given a specific amount of resources as input. Relating it to education, it means applying the most efficient option among different alternatives, to achieving the desired educational goals given an amount of educational resources (inputs).

In cost-effectiveness analysis, it is assumed that for a certain benefit or outcome to be desired, there are several alternative ways to achieve it. The basic question that cost-effectiveness analysis tries to answer is, "Which of these alternatives is the cheapest or most efficient way to get this benefit?" The procedures included in cost-effectiveness analysis consist of the following:

Setting the objective(s)

Cost-effectiveness analysis is designed to facilitate the attainment of certain goals or objectives. The objective must be set. Effectiveness is the measure of the extent to which this objective is achieved.

Identifying the alternatives

One of the most important steps in a cost-effectiveness analysis is to identify the relevant alternatives.

Analyzing the Costs

The costs associated with the alternatives must be estimated. The purpose is to estimate the costs associated with each alternative and to determine the degree to which each alternative may be effective in permitting the chosen objective to be reached.

Having a Decision Rule

The decision rule is a set of procedures that permits a choice to be made among alternatives on the basis of the cost and effectiveness of each.

Chapter Six

Cost-Benefit Analysis and Investment Decision Making in Education

The Concept of Cost-Benefit Analysis (CBA)

For both governments and individuals, the choice between different ways of investing resources rests to a great extent on an evaluation of the costs and benefits associated with the investments. One of the means through which costs and benefits associated with an investment are evaluated is the CBA.

The alternatives will differ as to the magnitude of the costs that must be incurred, the expected benefits that will be generated, the time scale of both costs and benefits, and the uncertainty or risks surrounding the project. The CBA is a technique by which these factors can be compared systematically for the purpose of evaluating the profitability of any proposed investment. The CBA is an aid to judgment that tries to evaluate both costs and benefits and to identify the investments that will achieve the greatest possible benefit in relation to cost. Samuel (1990) sees it as a technique that is directed at the evaluation of educational projects with a view to achieving optimality in the allocation of scarce resources.

In its analysis, the CBA takes the following parameters into account:

- assessing the profitability of a given investment by the size of the periodic monetary yield in relation to the original cost of investment;

- assessing the yield as a proportion of the costs of the asset in question; and
- estimating the internal rate that would equate the total yield from the particular investment to the original cost.

In essence, the general question that the CBA sets to answer is whether a number of investment projects should be undertaken and if the investible funds are limited, which one among the identified projects should qualify for selection. CBA, therefore, is a technique directed at the evaluation of investment projects with a view to achieving optimality in the allocation of scarce resources.

Cost-Benefit Analysis and Investment Decision Making in Education

The CBA approach emphasizes a systematic comparison of the magnitude of the costs and benefits of some forms of educational investment in order to determine the economic profitability of such investment.

CBA provides a rational model for investment decision making in education by relating the profitability of investment in one sector of the education enterprise to the other, or between various levels and types of education, such as technical, vocational, or science education.

CBA is an approach based on the social accounting model because it emphasizes rationality in investment decision making in education, as well as point the way for re-allocation of human and financial resources in education, if and when necessary. The principle of rationality in CBA is indeed vital for investment decision making in education for the following reasons:

- It helps to determine capital outlays in education.
- It assists in weighing the recurrent costs of education in relation to other sectors of the economy.

- It helps to relate the duration of a given course to the rate of returns.
- It assists in relating enrollments at each level of the educational system to cost implications.
- It explains the opportunity cost of a given educational program to the students or governments.

In making a choice therefore, the decision makers in education must relate the profitability of educational investment to its cost. Thus, CBA provides a rational model for investment decision making in education in terms of its emphasis on the need to achieve optimality in the allocation of scarce resources.

Mechanism of Cost-Benefit Analysis

The integral parts of CBA consist of the following:

1. The program to be implemented. Goals and targets (benefits) should be stated specifically.
2. There must be alternative investment opportunities for obtaining the set objective.
3. The opportunity cost on the investment or the program must be estimated.
4. There must be need to adopt mathematical model to assist in the estimation of benefit and cost as well as choice between alternative programs.
5. Social discount rate must be established to help select the best investment alternative.

Cost-Benefit Analysis Techniques

In cost-benefit analysis, the criterion reference is to select the alternative that yields the highest return. Three commonly used techniques are net present value (NPV), internal rate of return (IRR), and benefit-cost ratio. Other techniques are linear programming (LP) and information system (IS).

Net Present Value (NPV)

NPV is a technique that is often used to determine whether a program or project is worth investing in or not. It is the discounted monetary value of the expected net benefits of the project. To calculate NPV, the following steps are adopted:

1. monetary values are assigned to benefits and costs;
2. discount future benefits and costs using an appropriate discount rate; and
3. Subtract the sum total of the discounted costs from the sum total of the discounted benefits.

This will give NPV of the project. NPV is based on the principle that benefits accruing in the future are worth less than the same level of benefits that accrue now; furthermore, it takes the view that costs occurring now are more burdensome than costs that occur in the future. If the NPV is positive, then the financial return on the project is economically acceptable. If the NPV is negative, then the project is not acceptable in purely economic terms.

Calculation of Net Present Value

$$P = S_n \times \frac{1}{(1+r)^n} \quad \text{or} \quad \frac{S_n}{(1+r)^n}$$

P is the present value of a future sum of money, S_n

S_n = the sum to be received or the value of the total investment, after n years.

r = the rate of return, expressed as a proportion

n = the number of time periods (years) of the investment.

Exercises

Question

Calculate the present value of $60,000 at the end of year six, if a return of 15 percent per annum is obtainable.

Solution

$$PV = 60{,}000 \times \frac{1}{(1.15)^6}$$

$$= 60{,}000 \times 0.4323 = \$25{,}938$$

Question

How much would a person need to invest now at 12 percent to earn $4,000 at the end of both year two and year three?

Solution

$$PV = 4{,}000 \times \frac{1}{(1.12)^2} + 4{,}000 \times \frac{1}{(1.12)^3}$$

$$= 4{,}000 \times (0.7972 + 0.7118) = \$6{,}036$$

Question

Samriet Private School is considering whether to spend $5,000 on an item of equipment. The cash profits from the project would be in the first year $3,000 and in the second year $4,000. The school is not willing to invest in any project unless it offers a minimum return of 15 percent per annum. Is the project worthwhile?

Solution

Year	Cash flow $	Discount factor at 15%	Present value $
0	(5,000)	1.0	(5,000)
1	3,000	$\frac{1}{(1.15)^1} = 0.8696$	2,608.70
2	4,000	$\frac{1}{(1.15)^2} = 0.7561$	3,024.57
		Net Present Value	+ 633.27

$5,000 is the cost of the project. $3,000 is the expected cash profit in the first year and its present value now is $2,608.70. $4,000 is the expected cash profit in the second year and its present value now is $3,024.57. When we subtract the cost ($5,000) from the total cash profits ($2,608.70 + $3,024.57) at present value, we have positive net present value of $633.27. Since the value is positive, the project is worthwhile and the school can proceed to invest in it.

Question

An educational institution is wondering whether to spend $18,000 on an item of equipment in order to obtain cash profits of

Year	$
1	6,000
2	8,000
3	5,000
4	1,000

If the institution requires a return of 10 percent per annum, is the project viable?

Solution

Year	Cash flow $	Discount factor at 10%	Present value $
0	(18,000)	1.0	(18,000.0)
1	6,000	$\frac{1}{(1.10)^1} = 0.9091$	5,454.6
2	8,000	$\frac{1}{(1.10)^2} = 0.8264$	6,611.2
3	5,000	$\frac{1}{(1.10)^3} = 0.7513$	3,756.5
4	1,000	$\frac{1}{(1.10)^4} = 0.6830$	683.0
		Net present value	- 1,494.7

The NPV is negative, which means that the project is not viable and it is cheaper to invest elsewhere at 10 percent than to invest in the project. The project would earn a return of less than 10 percent.

Internal Rate of Return (IRR)

IRR is simply that rate of discount that equates the present value of benefits with the present value of costs.

PV of Benefits = PV of Costs

$$\sum_{t=o}^{n} \frac{B_t}{(1+r)^t} = \sum_{t=o}^{n.} \frac{C_t}{(1+r)^t}$$

Where r = internal rate of return
B_t = benefit in year t
C_t - cost in year t

Alternatively, IRR is the rate of interest (r) at which the difference between discounted benefits and costs is zero.

$$IRR = \sum_{t=o}^{n} \frac{B_t - C_t}{(1+r)^t} = O$$

This can further be expressed as follows:

$$IRR = \sum_{t=o}^{n} \frac{B_t}{(1+r)^t} - \sum_{t=o}^{n.} \frac{C_t}{(1+r)^t} = O$$

The higher a project's internal rate of return, the more desirable it is to undertake the project. The IRR is sometimes referred to as the economic rate of return (ERR). ERR implies the use of shadow prices and the calculation of a discount rate at which the benefits of the project equal the present costs, that is the economic net present value is equal to zero.

It is pertinent to draw a distinction between financial internal rate of return (FIRR) and EIRR. We speak of FIRR when the values are estimated at current prices, and EIRR when the values are estimated at shadow prices. Shadow prices are the opportunity costs of goods, usually different from the actual market prices and from regulated tariffs. Shadow price is often used as a synonym of accounting prices.

Calculation of Internal Rate of Return

Question

If an educational institution invests $5000 in a project today and $6000 is generated in a year's time, calculate the internal rate of return for the project.

Solution

PV of cost = PV of benefits

$$\frac{5000}{(1+r)^0} = \frac{6000}{(1+r)^1}$$

$$\frac{5000}{1} = \frac{6000}{(1+r)}$$

$$5000 = \frac{6000}{(1+r)}$$

$$5000\,(1+r) = 6000$$

$$1+r = \frac{6000}{5000}$$

$$1+r = 1.2$$

$$r = 1.2-1$$

$$r = 0.2$$

$$r = 20\%$$

The Internal Rate of Return = 20%

Question

If the same institution invests \$10,000 today and generates \$7,000 in the first year and \$6000 in the second year, what will be the internal rate of return for the project?

Solution

PV of Cost = PV of benefits

$$\frac{10{,}000}{(1+r)^0} = \frac{7000}{(1+r)^1} + \frac{6000}{(1+r)^2}$$

$$10{,}000 = \frac{7000}{(1+r)} + \frac{6000}{(1+r)^2}$$

Multiplying both sides by $(1 + r)^2$

$$10{,}000\,(1 + r)^2 = 7000(1 + r) + 6000$$

$$10{,}000\,(1 + r)(1 + r) = 7000 + 7000r + 6000$$

$$10{,}000\,(1 + r + r + r^2) = 7000 + 7000r + 6000$$

$$10{,}000\,(1 + 2r + r^2) = 7000 + 7000r + 6000$$

$$10{,}000 + 20{,}000r + 10{,}000r^2 = 7000 + 7000r + 6000$$

$$10{,}000 + 20{,}000r + 10{,}000r^2 = 13000 + 7000r$$

$$10{,}000r^2 + 13{,}000r - 3000 = 0$$

$$10r^2 + 13r - 3 = 0$$

$$r = \frac{-13 \pm \sqrt{169 - 4(10)(-3)}}{20}$$

$$= \frac{-13 - 17}{20} \text{ or } \frac{-13 + 17}{20}$$

$$= -1.5 \text{ or } +0.2$$

$$= -150\% \text{ or } 20\%$$

Since high negative return is not a practical preposition, r = 20 percent. Internal rate of return = 20 percent

Calculating Internal Rate of Return by Interpolation Method

This method demands that the IRR is calculated by first finding two interest rates (discount rates) which give an NPV close to zero. One interest rate should give a positive NPV and the other a negative NPV. The IRR would then be somewhere between these two interest rates (above the rate where the NPV is positive, but below the rate where the NPV is negative).

$$IRR = r_1 + \frac{P_1}{P_1 - P_2}(r_2 - r_1)$$

Where r_1 and r_2 are the first and second interest rates respectively; r_1 is the lower interest rate and r_2 is the higher interest rate). P_1 is the NPV (positive) at the lower rate, r_1. P_2 is the NPV (negative) at the higher rate, r_2.

Question

A project costing $8,000 in year O is expected to earn $4,000 in year one, $3000 in year two, and $2000 in year three. What is the internal rate of return?

Solution

Although much guesswork is involved to start this procedure, but a very rough guideline for determining the interest rate at which the NPV might be close to zero, is to apply the formula stated below:

$$2/3 \times \left(\frac{\text{Profit}}{\text{Cost of the project}}\right)$$

In our example, the total profit over three years is ($4,000 + $3,000 + $2,000 – $8,000) = $1000

$$2/3 \times \frac{1000}{8000} = 0.08 \text{ approx.}$$

$$= 8\%$$

A starting point is to try 8 percent.

Try 8%

Year	Cash flow $	Discount factor at 8%	Present value $
0	(8,000)	1.000	(8,000)
1	4,000	$\frac{1}{(1.08)^1} = 0.9259$	3703.6
2	3,000	$\frac{1}{(1.08)^2} = 0.8573$	2571.9
3	2,000	$\frac{1}{(1.08)^3} = 0.7938$	1587.6
		Net present value	= – 136.9

The NPV is negative, therefore the project fails to earn 8 percent and the IRR must be less than 8 percent.

Try 6%

Year	Cash flow $	Discount factor at 6%	Present value $
0	(8,000)	1.000	(8,000)
1	4,000	$\frac{1}{(1.06)^1} = 0.9434$	3773.6
2	3,000	$\frac{1}{(1.06)^2} = 0.8900$	2670.0
3	2,000	$\frac{1}{(1.06)^3} = 0.8396$	1679.2
		Net present value	= + 122.80

The NPV is positive, therefore the project earns more than 6 percent and less than 8 percent.

Calculation by interpolation:

$$\text{IRR} = r_1 + \frac{P_1}{P_1 - P_2}(r_2 - r_1)$$

$$= 6\% + \left(\frac{122.8}{122.8 - (-136.9)} \text{ x } (8-6)\%\right)$$

$$= 6\% + \left(\frac{122.8}{122.8 + 136.9} \text{ x } 2\%\right)$$

$$= 6\% + \left(\frac{122.8}{259.7} \text{ x } 2\%\right)$$

$$= 6 + 0.95\%$$

$$= 6.95\% \text{ (approx.).}$$

$$\text{IRR} = 6.95\%$$

Benefit Cost Ratio

This is one of the techniques in appraising the profitability of an investment. Benefit cost ratio presumes that if the ratio of benefit and cost of a proposed investment is greater than one, the investment should be embarked upon.

$$\text{BCR} = \frac{\Sigma B_t}{\Sigma C_t} > 1$$

Where BCR = Benefit Cost Ratio. B_t = Economic Benefit from education in year t. C_t = cost of education in year t.

The major weakness this approach has is that it does not take into consideration the effect of inflation on the value of money.

Calculation of Benefit Cost Ratio

Question

An educational institution is willing to embark on a training program that costs \$500,000 for a period of four years, and it expects \$180,000, \$190,000, \$200,000 and \$220,000 as returns for the four years respectively. Is the project viable?

Solution

$$BCR = \frac{\sum B_t}{\sum C_t}$$

Where BCR = Benefit – Cost Ratio. $\sum B_t$ = total economic benefits at end of the period. $\sum C_t$ = total costs of the program at end of the period.

$$\text{Therefore, BCR} = \frac{\$790{,}000}{\$500{,}000} = 1.58$$

Since the profitability criterion says the ratio must be greater than one, the project is viable.

Other techniques associated with Cost-Benefit Analysis (CBA) are the following :

Linear Programming (LP): This is a general mathematical model. It can be used to allocate scarce resources among competing activities given constraints in order to maximize the attainment of set objectives.

Information System: This ensures regular information flow in respect of cost benefit and time operation of economy for the purpose of CBA. Other techniques are Program Curve Analysis and Engineering Analysis.

The Application of CBA and Economics of Education

CBA is useful as a basis of deciding on investment decision. It provides a basis for social calculation generally referred to as shadow prices different from market prices.

From the macro point of view, it provides a rational framework for choosing among alternative programs considering national objectives and values. Thus, whether to invest more in agriculture, health, or rural electrification depends on a national parameter that has significant optimal utilization of natural resources. CBA guides decision makers in getting their priorities right.

At the micro level, Oguntoye and Alani (1998) stress that CBA is useful in allocating space and helping teachers to provide school efficiency. Hatry (Oguntoye and Alani, 1998) has suggested that the technique can be used to, "Make decisions in situations where scarcity of resources is a problem in selecting among alternatives; provide directions as to the areas for research in which funds might be applied to bring overall system savings or to reduce areas of uncertainty; and suggest additional alternatives that could be used in the face of the major difficulties experienced with the examined alternatives" (60).

It is the CBA approach that helps us to embark on a systematic comparison of the magnitude of the cost and benefit of some forms of educational investment in order to determine the economic profitability of such investment. Through the application of CBA, educational wastages can be reduced to a minimal level. It is observed that wastages increase the social costs of education without correspondingly increasing the benefits. When investment in education is subjected to CBA, wastages are reduced.

Problems of CBA

CBA analysis does not identify externalities (spillover benefits) such as technological, innovational, and intergenerational effects. Aside, it is unreliable as a guide for fundamental structural changes in the pattern of investment. It also ignores the political nature of decision making in education. What is economically rational may not be politically rational.

Other objections are raised with respect to use of discount rate period of time for calculating rates and the alternative against which the program is being selected. This means that CBA cannot be used without selecting a discount rate, so the values of the criteria depend on the choice of discount rate.

Conclusion

The concept, mechanism, application, and problems of CBA have been examined. Despite its problems, CBA in education allows educational managers and policy makers to consider the available data in order to estimate the costs and benefits before making decisions rather than using the rule of the thumb in making decision.

Chapter Seven

Efficiency in Education

Efficiency in Education generally refers to the capacity of an educational system to turn its products (students) out with minimum wastage. In other words, efficiency in education means the ability of an educational system to achieve the desired results (outputs) with a minimum application of resources (inputs). Efficiency in Education can be categorized internally, externally, technically, and economically.

Internal Efficiency in Education

Internal efficiency refers to the relationship between a system's outputs (learning achievements) and the corresponding inputs that went into creating them. It refers to the extent to which an educational system is able to minimize the number of years a pupil or student spends before successfully completing an educational program. In other words, it is the degree to which repetition, dropout and failure, as wastage indicators can be minimized.

For example, a primary school system is rated as highly inefficient, if half the pupils who enroll in grade one drop out before completing grade six, and if, in addition, the average completer repeats two grades along the way, taking eight years instead of six to finish the cycle. By this definition, a school system with no dropouts or repeaters would be 100 percent efficient (Coombs and Hallak, 1987).

An educational system is internally efficient if and only if output (outcomes) can be sustained or increased with minimal input. In other words, internal efficiency relates to increased outcomes or outputs at constant or reduced inputs.

External Efficiency in Education

External efficiency refers to the relationship between the cost of producing outputs in a particular period and the cumulative benefits that subsequently accrue from that outputs over a longer period of time. The benefits might be individual, social, economic, or non-economic benefits.

An educational system is externally efficient if and when the outputs (products) of the system are employed in the labor market. An educational system is externally inefficient if the services of what it turns out as products are not relevant to the economy's manpower needs and employment opportunities. The system is also externally inefficient if its products lack the prerequisite skills for the labor market.

The system might also have produced well-trained specialists, but if too few jobs are available for them in that field, the investment in their training is likely to produce few benefits. The same resources devoted to training more of the specialists needed by the country would be far more efficient or productive.

Technical Efficiency in Education

This is a concept that explains that the products of a given educational system should be gainfully utilized provided such products are ready to justify their pay package, all things being equal.

This concept explains why workers in private establishments such as banks and oil companies are paid handsome salaries. The notion is that the workers in these establishments are fully utilized, and they are paid due to their technical efficiency.

In the same vein, it is also technically efficient for the educational institutions to utilize their facilities, including teaching and non-teaching staff.

Economic Efficiency in Education

This refers to increasing the output or outcomes (learning results) of an educational system without increasing the cost of production. For example, when the number of teachers, facilities and other inputs remain constant while outputs increase, the educational system is economically efficient.

Education and Development

Concept of Education

When we are talking about the term education, the first thing that readily comes to our mind is school. We forget that there was education long before there were schools and teachers inside of them. Education is taken to mean only an activity that has direct links with the schools. The word education transcends the notion of activity taking place in schools. In fact, the grown-up members of a community have educated the younger ones ever since the dawn of history. And, we remember that such of education under many different guises happens outside schools. Mothers and fathers teach their children how to speak their language; older children learn some of whatever the adults are doing by seeing it being done, and travelled members of the community may teach their neighbors what they have learned elsewhere. When we start to think about it, we see that education can happen in many lively and colorful ways.

Education, therefore, is the process of transmitting ideas, cultural values, skills, and knowledge from experienced person to inexperienced person.

Yet, education everywhere nowadays can hardly function without being planned. This is how we come about educational planning. No society ever has been completely static. These kinds of change we have come to observe in more recent times show a formerly unknown face. Aside, there is man's determination to make changes happen rather than to preserve the old ways. And so, there is the great speed of change in the societies.

Rapid social change has one particularly serious consequence: the knowledge that helped parents to lead a successful life in their surroundings is in danger of being more or less useless to their children, since the surroundings have changed drastically. Thus, much of informal education, of education outside and beside school, is in danger of losing its function. The new generation tends to become, for better or worse, more and more dependent on the school (on the official "educational system"). And such a system needs to be planned, if it is to keep up with a changing society.

Concept of Development

The notion that society is changing because there are people who want to see changes happen in it is similar to saying that development is dependent on the conscious effort of people. That means that development does not happen automatically and those who want change want only specific kinds of change that lead to development.

What then is Development? Looking at the original meaning of the word development, it refers to a process we can observe as something happening naturally. Development is a term that was initially used by biologists as a name for the process that, for example, turns an egg into a chicken or a tomato seed into a tomato plant. In this case, we need not to worry about the outcome; nature makes sure that chicken eggs turn into chickens rather vultures. Developments in society, nations, culture, and education, however, cannot be guaranteed by nature. Man is responsible for them. It is the efforts of the people that are put together to improve the well-being of the society itself. In this case, development means improvement in the living conditions of people in the society.

Development in a general characterization, therefore, refers to a purposeful process initiated by man in order to improve the well-being of those living together in a society.

When we talk of development, three important requirements are necessary for it:

1. It has to be a process that improves well-being.
2. The process has to be initiated by man; and
3. The process has to be kept going. Thus, we have to stay with it and see to it that the actions we have planned are really undertaken. We need to administer and manage development.

Indicators of Development

Development may show itself in many ways. For example, when we have development, there will be more new things and institutions, roads, hospitals, schools, farm machinery, factories, electricity lines, telephone lines, etc. All these can be taken as indicators of development. In a more precise way, indicators of development are discussed below:

Growth

Growth is an indicator of development in any society. Growth is something that can be expressed in quantitative terms. An indicator is the one that gives us a quantitative description of developments in various fields of a country's development. The one indicator most then used in studying a country's development over time and in comparing countries among each other is the one that stands for the overall performance of a country's economy, that is the GNP. It is a very useful indicator of development.

GNP is defined as the total value of a nation's annual output of goods and services. Since the GNP is all-comprehensive and readily available for virtually any country, it is the indicator most commonly used for observing a country's performance over time and with certain adjustments for comparing countries among each others.

Since GNP measures the total value of a nation's production of goods and services, we may expect that in a country with a population of 100 million people, much more is produced than in a country with only 10 million people.

Another indicator under growth is per capita income. This is an indicator derived from the GNP. Per capita income relates the GNP to the size of a country's population. It is only a very rough measure for people's well-being. For the per capita income to grow at all, the GNP must grow at least as fast as the population.

The growth from one year to the next is expressed as the annual growth rate (r_n) and given as a percentage figure with help of the following calculation:

$$Rn = \frac{GNPn - 1}{GNP_{n-1}} \times 100$$

Where GNP_n = GNP for the year n

Rn = Annual growth rate of GNP from year n-1 to year n.

Per Capita Income is obtained by dividing a country's GNP by its population.

$$\text{Per Capita Income} = \frac{\text{GNP (Y)}}{\text{Population (p)}}$$

Table: GNP, per capita income, population and growth rates

	GNP	Population	Per capita income	Annual rate	Growth (%)
Country				Population	Per capita income (real)
	(1)	(2)	(3)	(4)	(5)
Afghanistan	2,290	14,616	160	2.2	2.7
Bangladesh	7,280	84,655	90	2.8	0.2
Brazil	180,020	119,461	1510	2.9	6.0
Cuba	12,330	9,728	1270	1.6	4.7
Denmark	60,830	5,106	10580	0.4	2.7
Ecuador	7,400	7,814	950	3.3	5.6
Haiti	1,150	4,831	240	1.7	2.2
Hungary	37,150	10,685	3480	0.4	5.1
India	117,520	643,896	180	2.0	1.6
Malaysia	15,270	13,300	1150	2.7	4.8
Mexico	91,910	65,442	1400	3.3	1.3
Netherlands	128,270	13,937	9200	0.8	2.3
New Zealand	17,700	3,201	5530	1.7	0.9
Romania	36,190	21,872	1650	0.9	9.6
Sri Lanka	2,870	14,346	200	1.9	1.7
Sudan	5,900	17,376	340	2.7	2.6
Sweden	87,260	8,277	10540	0.3	2.1
Thailand	23,390	44,517	530	2.8	4.5
Venezuela	49,880	13,973	2850	3.4	3.1
Zambia	2,720	5,291	510	3.1	-0.9

Source: 1980 World Bank Atlas: populations, per capita product and growth rates.

Quality of Life

The question to ask here is: what other evidence one can point to in order to assess whether development has taken place or not. This evidence is the quality of life of people in a society.

By quality of life, we mean that aspect of development that deals with distribution, equality, and the state of health of a society. Usually, such indicators are summarily referred to as socio-economic indicators.

According to the Research Institute of the United Nations (1970), the core indicators of socio-economic development are as follows:

1. Expectation of life at birth
2. Percent population in localities is 20,000 and over
3. Consumption of animal protein, per day
4. Combined primary and secondary school enrollment
5. Vocational enrollment ratio
6. Average number of people per room
7. Newspaper circulation per 1,000 population
8. Percentage of economically active population in electricity, gas, water, etc.
9. Agricultural production per male agricultural worker
10. Percent percentage of adult male labor in agriculture
11. Electricity consumption, kilowatts per hour per capita
12. Steel consumption, kilograms per capita
13. Energy consumption, kilograms of coal equivalent per capita
14. Percent GDP derived from manufacturing
15. Foreign trade per capita, in United States dollars
16. Percent salaries and wage earners to total economically active population.

Conclusion

Under education and development, the concepts of education and development have been discussed in the societal context. The indicators of development have also been assessed.

As earlier on mentioned, without qualitative education, there can be no development. Any aspect of development in any country is a function of education. And so, our educational system needs to be well planned based on the needs and aspirations of the country. That is, there is a need for our policy makers, administrators, and decision makers to plan a worthwhile education towards the development of the country.

Aside, Education clearly has indirect as well as direct effects on economic development because of its influence on the structure of society—notably by promoting social and occupational mobility—its effect upon the climate for enterprise and its contribution to the productivity of the workers. It also provides the basis for the creation of democratic societies where political power is broadly based. At certain stages of a country's development there may be the cause of social tensions, since education creates new aspirations and widens horizons for both individuals and countries. At other junctures, it may be precisely the force that relieves tensions and creates understanding, not only within different groups and classes within the country, but also on international scale.

Chapter Eight

Educational Finance

Introduction

Interest in the financial aspects of education today is growing. One of the reasons advanced for this development is the considerable growth in the volume of educational activity to the point where education is easily one of the largest industries in virtually all countries. In Nigeria and the United States, education is the chief employer of highly skilled personnel. According to O'Donoghue (1971), education utilizes large amounts of a country's available resources and affects the well-being of the population. One of the resources that education utilizes is money, and this is a very important input on which the success of any school system depends. In virtually all countries, public expenditures on education have been rising not only in absolute terms but also as a percentage of GNP, national income, and total public revenues (Ogbodo, 1995).

Educational finance refers to the process of procuring and disbursing of financial resources meant for the provision of education of a given standard stipulated by a community or society.

The financing of education has been an interaction problem for government in most countries of the world, especially in the developing countries because of the uncontrolled population explosion in schools.

This chapter, therefore, focuses on educational systems of Nigeria and the United States. It is to bring out the similarities and otherwise in educational finance of these countries noting the structural-functionalism of their economies and politics.

The Economy and Politics of Nigeria

Nigeria is located in West Africa with a total land area of 923,768 square kilometers, extending 1,127 kilometers east to west and 1,046 kilometers north to south (*Encyclopedia of the Third World*, 1978). Nigeria is structurally a populous country with many ethnic groups. No group enjoys an absolute numerical majority, but the three dominant ethnic groups are Igbo, Hausa, and Yoruba. The official language is English. Nigeria is one of the low-income countries of the world with a free-market economy based on oil and dominated by the private sector. Politically, it practices federalism with a democratic government put in place. At present, it has thirty-six states, which are independent of one another politically. Nigeria is endowed with natural resources such as water, livestock, forest products, substantial wild life, and ample fishery resources; human resources in the form of skilled, semi-skilled, and unskilled labor forces; industrial resources such as basic agro-industries and mineral resources; and infrastructural resources such as access roads, power in terms of electricity, water supply, and railways (Akinyemi, 1999).

The Economy and Politics of the United States

The United States is a vast country, the fourth largest country in the world with area of about 3,615,211 square miles (Finer, 1982). The United States society is open-ended, with neither a ruling elite at its top nor a working class at its base. The country comprises a large number of somewhat divisible vertical sub-cultures living side by side and mingling largely by inter-marriage and migration. The United States practices federalism, which emanated from a very loose geographical bond and recognition given to localism. This means that there is a division of the functions of government between the center, represented by the national government, and the localities, represented by the state governments. The federal and the state governments are based upon the principle of separation of powers. This enables one bit of the government to say something different from the other bit. Another governmental feature is the remarkably loose structure of the two main political parties and their lack of coherent program or ideologies.

Nigeria's Educational System

Nigeria's educational system has passed through many changes, innovations, and reforms since the attainment of political independence in 1960. It was subject to several reviews such as Banjo Review, the Taiwo Review, the Ikoku Review, the Diko Review, and many others immediately after independence (Oyedeji, 1983). The universal primary education (UPE) introduced in the defunct western and eastern Regions in 1955 and 1957 respectively was reintroduced in 1976 and yielded little or no viable results. This means that the scheme did not achieve the set goals. The year 1977 experienced the launching of the National Policy on Education, which was revised in 1981. This policy ushered in a new system of education, the 6-3-3-4 that replaced the old system, 6-5-2-3, because of its weaknesses and inadequacies. Presently, the 6-3-3-4 has given way to the new universal basic education (UBE), which is being implemented.

In Nigeria, the educational system is divided into various levels. These levels are represented in hierarchical order in Figure 1.

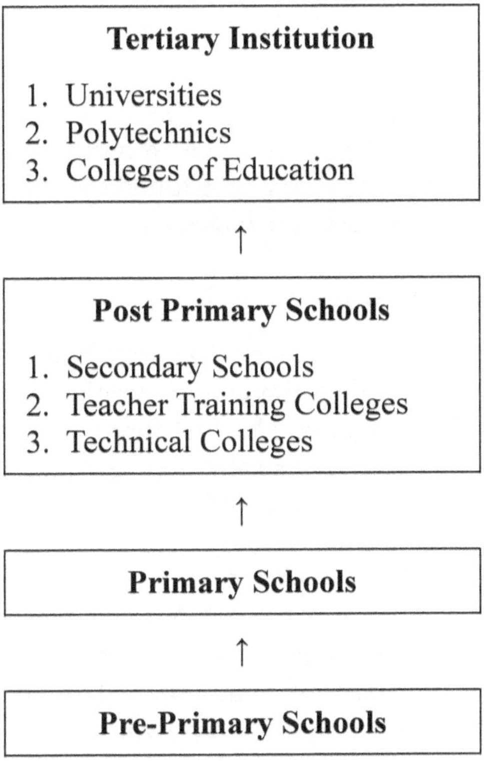

Tertiary Institution

1. Universities
2. Polytechnics
3. Colleges of Education

↑

Post Primary Schools

1. Secondary Schools
2. Teacher Training Colleges
3. Technical Colleges

↑

Primary Schools

↑

Pre-Primary Schools

At the lowest level are the pre-primary schools, followed by the primary schools. Next are the post-primary schools. Finally, we have the tertiary institutions.

Pre-Primary Education in Nigeria

Pre-primary education in Nigeria is known as kindergarten or nursery schools. It usually admits children ages three through five. Most of these schools are owned and financed by private individuals. Children who are sent to these schools are not primarily sent to acquire any tangible knowledge, but to relieve their mothers especially of talking all day (Omokhodion, 1995).

Primary Education in Nigeria

This comprises the first six years in the UBE program in the Nigerian educational system. At this level, children of age six years get enrolled for a six-year program. This is because primary education is taken to be the foundation on which the rest of the educational system and stages are built.

Secondary Education

This type of education is six years in duration and is given in two parts, with a part having a three-year duration of the remaining compulsory UBE program. The first three years that represent part of UBE are the compulsory junior secondary school (JSS) education, while the last three years represent senior secondary education.

The junior secondary education is both pre-vocational and academic, while the senior secondary is for those who are able and willing to have a complete six-year education. The aim is that successful graduates of junior secondary education would proceed to senior secondary education, while those who could not pass the JSS examination would have to get into the vocational training streams (Omokhodion 1998). Thus, we have trade centers and technical colleges, which cater for vocational training.

Vocational and Technical Education

According to the National Policy of Education (2004), technical education aims at providing manpower in applied technology, commerce, and vocational skills necessary for agricultural, industrial, commercial and economic development. This type of education is provided by technical colleges and trade centers.

Teacher Training Colleges

The third type of secondary is the grade two teacher training colleges. Most of these colleges have faded away; however, there are some that are still operational. The most notable one is Nigeria Teachers Institute (NTI), which has a base in Kaduna, but has branches all over the nation.

Tertiary Education

Tertiary Education as defined in the National Policy on Education (1981) covers the post-secondary section of the national education system that is given in universities, polytechnics, colleges of technology and colleges of education. Education at this level is given to train middle and high level manpower for national development. This goal is expected to be pursued through teaching, research, the dissemination of existing and new information, and service to the community (National Policy on Education 2004).

United States' Educational System

The educational system of the United States evolved largely as a result of the influence of the early colonists from England, Scotland, Holland, France, and Spain (Omokhodion 1995). One of the most salient features of the school system in United States is the absence of national administration. That is, each of the states that constitute United States controls and directs its own schools. Other important features are 1) the absence of fees in elementary and secondary schools and in some cases in higher institutions, 2) the separation of church and state in educational affairs, and 3) compulsory school attendance until the age of sixteen (Omokhodion 1995).

The educational system of United States is divided into three different levels: elementary education, secondary education, and higher education.

Elementary Education

This refers to the basic or introductory schooling that children receive, usually beginning at the age of six. At this level, learning experiences are organized to inculcate in children respect for the rights of others, acceptance of social responsibilities, and cooperation with others in the society. Kindergarten through grade five or six comprises this level.

Secondary Education

Secondary education in the United States is classified into three major categories according to program:

1. A high school encompassing grades nine through twelve. This involves a comprehensive school that is open to all youths of a community or attendance area.
2. A vocational school, which is for students of a community who are interested in its specialized area of training, and
3. A specialized high school that is for pupils with special capabilities and who in addition are qualified to concentrate on a particular area of study. This involves the high schools for pupils that are talented academically, musically, artistically or mechanically.

Higher Education

In the United States, there are two different systems of higher education, namely:

1. State universities and colleges, maintained and subsidized by the states, but some fees are paid by their attendees;
2. Fee institutions, independent universities and colleges maintained by various churches or private foundations, charging rather high fees.

Educational Finance in Nigeria

Financing education in Nigeria dates back to the year 1842, when the missionaries saw the need to provide education for the people and there was the need to expend money on it. The urge to standardize education in the country prompted the government to get involved in the provision of education and it initially granted aids to the missionary schools that met specified needs and provided scholarship for few deserving students. Later, financial involvement of government increased.

Historically, financing education in Nigeria was accomplished through three sources: 1) grant-in-aids from government, 2) collection of fees, and 3) levies by cultural union or voluntary contribution by parents and guardians.

Today, financing education has taken a new dimension that is called a dual system of financing; government expenditure and private contributions in forms of fees and individual donors. At present, education is being financed through the following means, among others:

Budgetary Allocation

All tiers of government annually make budgetary allocations to education. This allocation constitutes a major source of school finance in Nigeria. Public educational institutions at all levels are financed this way. For example, Lagos State budgetary allocation is as follows:

Total budgetary allocation to primary and post primary education in Lagos State (1995–1999)

Years	Capital Expenditure	Recurrent Expenditure	Total Expenditure
1995	N120,321,454	N417,632,827	N537,954,370
1996	N200,668,101	N716,038,809	N916,706,910
1997	N258,144,433	N959,449,472	N1,217,593,905
1998	N315,727,117	N1,031,088,374	N1,346,815,491
1999	N429,008,215	N1,179,428,505	N1,608,436,720

Source: Lagos State Teaching Service Commission Old Secretariat, Ikeja.

Education Tax Funds (ETF)

In response to the recommendations of some concerned groups in society, the government promulgated the Education Tax Decree of 1993 to raise funds for the education sector. This is in realization that the private sector as the main beneficiary of the products of education should directly share in the burden of its finance.

The decree provides for the following:

- That companies are to pay 2 percent of their profits to the education fund.
- That the fund is to be managed and disbursed by a special tax board of trustees of the Federal Inland Revenue Department.
- That the fund would be used to finance development of work houses, procurement of books and library facilities, and the purchase and maintenance of equipment.
- That 50 percent is for tertiary institutions, 25 percent is for the universities, while 25 percent would be shared by polytechnics and colleges of education on pro-rata basis. The remaining 50 percent of the fund would be shared among primary and post primary institutions. Primary institutions would take three-eighths of the fund (Ogbodo, 1995).

School Fees

Tuition fees are paid in some states at the secondary and tertiary institutions. Other fees such as accommodations and meal fees are also paid. These represent considerable private contribution to education finance in the country.

PTA Levies

The individual schools' funds collected through approved levies of PTAs help in meeting some needs especially in the area of capital development. According to Ogbodo (1998), many public primary and secondary schools rely on such contributions for the erection of classroom blocks, staff quarters, fencing, and other such needs.

External Financing

Several foreign donor agencies have continued to support educational programs in Nigeria. Such foreign donor agencies are United Nations International Children's Emergency Fund (UNICEF) which is donating towards the Early Child Care Development and Education (ECCDE) project in Nigeria; the World Bank, which is assisting in the education of the country through the World Bank Assisted Funds and programs (such as the World Bank Assisted Primary Education Project and the World Bank Assisted Universities project); United Nations Development Programme (UNDP), which assists Nigerian education through staff development, provision of equipment and materials, and development of software. UNESCO is providing technical advisory support for the program, while UNICEF also contributes to it mainly in the area of women's and girls' education. Today, the basic education for all program has become the highest priority for donor assistance.

Student Aid Programs

Governments do provide cheap loans to indigent students to enable them finance their education. For example, the establishment of scholarship boards is serving this purpose.

Educational Finance In The United States

The United States, like Nigeria, is a federal state with fifty independent states and several additional territories. As far as education finance is concerned, the state governments provide the largest share of educational funds, while the local school districts provide the rest; this varies from state to state. The federal government provides just a fractional part of total elementary and secondary public funding. Most of the funds it provides are targeted at compensatory and remedial education.

In the United States, Education is financed through several different means.

Federal Funds

The federal government provides funds for education, but only a very small fraction of the needed education funds. Most of the federal funds are directed towards special populations and programs that foster equal access and opportunity, such as those for the disadvantaged, the handicapped, and women.

Taxes on Sales, Usages, and Income

The revenues generated through these means by the states are tied to education. The so-called sin taxes on alcohol, tobacco, and lottery or gambling proceeds are also devoted to education by the states. Thus, the state governments provide the largest share of educational funds. Also, the major share of any new educational funds comes from the state sources.

Property Taxes

These are the best known source of funds for education at the local level. Despite the trend towards more state funding and control, local school boards, administrators, teachers, and parents are more sophisticated about the processes of education today than at any other time. The decisions about school organization and management are best made at the local level. It is the local communities that collect property taxes, and the greater part of these taxes is devoted to education through local school districts.

Tuition and Fees

These are another sources of financing education in United States, private schools charge tuition and fees for the services being rendered by them. This is common in higher institutions of learning.

Business Role in Financing Education

Financing public education is a public responsibility through local, state, and federal mechanisms. In the United States, businesses are not financiers of public education in any substantial way except as taxpayers. The only way businesses get involved with schools and school systems is through partnerships and other collaborative activities. This never represents a major source of funds for the schools.

Similarities in the Mode of Educational Finance between Nigeria and the United States

Government Funding of Education

All the tiers of government in both Nigeria and the United States make allocations to education. In Nigeria, federal and state governments make budgetary allocations to public educational institutions at all levels, while local governments provide for only primary schools. In the United States, federal, states, and local communities finance public educational institutions at all levels.

Financing Education Through Taxes

These two countries also finance education through taxes. In Nigeria, there is an education tax that demands that companies are to pay 2 percent of their profits to the education fund. This tax is used to finance education at all levels. In the United States, sin taxes are charged on alcohol, tobacco, and lottery or gambling proceeds at the state level, and they are devoted to education. Also at the local level, property tax is charged and this constitutes a major source of educational finance in the local education districts.

Table 2 Institutions of Higher Education Finances: 1975–1986 (in millions of dollars)

Items	1975	1980	1982	1983	1984	1985	1986 public	Private
tuition and fees	7,233	11,930	15,774	17,776	19,715	21,283	9,439	13,677
fed. govt.	4,991	7,772	8,320	8,181	8,783	9,615	6,699	3,767
state govt.	10,857	18,378	21,849	23,066	24,707	27,583	29,221	691
local govt.	1,424	1,588	1,938	2,031	2,387	2,545	2,326	219
endowment earnings	718	1,177	1,597	1,874	2,096	398	1,877	
private gifts & grants	1,745	2,808	3,564	4,059	4,415	4,896	2,110	3,301
auxiliary enterprises	4,080	6,481	8,122	8,770	9,456	10,100	6,685	3,989

Source: United States Department of Education, Digest of Education Statistics.

Table 2 shows the roles of the government institutions, schools, and private sources in financing education in United States. From the table, it is clearly revealed that the states carry the lion's share of the educational finance.

Tuitions and Fees

In Nigeria, tuition and fees are paid in some states at the secondary and tertiary institutions. In the United States, tuitions and fees are paid in the private primary and secondary educational institutions, as well as at all tertiary institutions. These tuitions and fees represent considerable private contributions to education in the two countries.

Private Grants

In Nigeria, private individuals such as philanthropic donors and PTAs finance education through grants, donations, and scholarship. In the United States, the same thing is applicable. Private individuals finance education through gifts and grants. This is evident in the Table 2.

Contrasts in the Mode of Educational Finance Between Nigeria and the United States

- In Nigeria, the federal government provides the largest share of educational funds while the state and the local governments provide the rest, unlike the United States where the state governments provide the largest share of educational funds, and the local school districts provide the rest.
- The Nigerian educational system provides for approved educational levies, which are collected through recognized PTAs. These levies help in the area of capital development such as the erection of classroom blocks, fencing, staff quarters, and libraries. In the United States, there is no provision for such levies. The only levies relied upon come from taxes that are devoted to education.
- External financing is provided through several foreign donor agencies such as UNICEF, World

Bank, and UNDP. The United States is self-sufficient as far as educational financing is concerned; they do not seek the assistance of foreign donor agencies in the areas of educational financing.

- The business role in educational finance: In the United States, educational finance is the responsibility of the governments. The business world is not a financier of public education, but only gets involved as a taxpayer. In Nigeria, the private sector and the business world are co-opted into the financing of education since they are also the beneficiaries of the products of education.

Education finance of Nigeria and the United States, being the countries that practice federalism, has been assessed, compared, and contrasted. The two countries have similar modes of educational finance in government funding, education taxes, tuition and fees, and private grants. The share of the educational finance formula, external financing, and private involvement in financing education is where they differ.

Various forms of Public Support for Education in Nigeria

The Nigerian educational system gets its public support for education through various forms. These sources of funds are listed below:

1. Parent Teacher Associations (PTA)
2. Alumni associations
3. Educational development levy
4. Examination Fees
5. External Aid from organizations such as UNICEF, UNESCO, UNDP/WORLD BANK, USAID
6. Voluntary Organizations such as the Rotary Club and the Lions Club

7. Community development programs, i.e., fund raising and property taxes
8. Philanthropists
9. Government workers' annual educational development levy
10. Companies' donations from places such as Chevron, Shell Petroleum, VAT, and ETF

Indices Influencing Financial Allocation to Education

There are certain factors that influence GNP and budgetary ratios allocated to education. These factors, among others are the following:

Literacy/Illiteracy Rates

Basically, most countries with high illiteracy rates are likely to allocate more money to education than most literacy societies. This is because reduction in the level of illiteracy can go a long way to banish ignorance, poverty, socio-political maladjustments, and so on. In essence, it helps to empower individual consumers for education; however, some literate societies also spend more money on education depending on the goals and aspirations of the economy, particularly on the types of job.

Salaries and allowances of teachers and other members of Educational Staff

The education sector is the largest employer of personnel. The salaries and allowances of educational personnel gulp a greater percentage of budgetary allocation to education than in any other country. In research conducted by Akinyemi (2005) on the analysis of unit costs of public primary education in Lagos State of Nigeria, it was found that more 70 percent of the budgetary allocation to education was gulped by wage bills of personnel, while less than 30 percent was expended on capital project. Because of the number of personnel involved in education sectors, more money will have to be allocated.

Level of Technology

While most developed economies can rely on their levels of technological sophistication, the developing nations cannot. For example, developed economies can produce science and technological equipment for education, while developing nations cannot. This will call for financial allocation to procure necessary equipment to foster a higher level of technology in the developing countries.

The Schooling Age

In most developing countries of the world, a larger percentage of their young boys and girls fall within school age and government must provide for their education.

The Meaning of Underfunding of Education

Underfunding is one of the tortuous problems preventing the education sector from translating its policy goals to meaningful reality. Samuel (1994) conceptualizes underfunding of education as a gap between investment required for proper funding of education and actual resources made available for education. In a technical term, underfunding of education means non-correlation between demand and supply of money to education. In this case, financial resources demanded outstrip the financial resources supplied into education sector. In operational terms, a country's education is underfunded if what it (that country) devotes to its education out of its annual budget is less that the UNESCO's recommendation of 26 percent of GDP for education. Furthermore, that country has poor funding of education if what it devotes to its education is less than 15 percent.

The table below best describes underfunding and poor funding of countries' education.

Table 3 Percentage of Central Government Expenditure

Allocation to Education (1986–1992)

Countries	Percentage of GDP allocated to Education
Angola	15
Botswana	21
Brazil	21
Cameroon	12
Egypt	13
Ghana	26
Indonesia	9
Iran Islamic Republic	21
Jordan	15
Kenya	2
Kuwait	20
Malaysia	19
Morocco	17
Namibia	22
Nigeria	3
Tunisia	17
Turkey	18
UAE	15
Uganda	15

Source: United Nations International Children's Emergency Fund (UNICEF) report, 1995

According to the table, Ghana was the only country that had the UNESCO's recommended 26 percent of GDP for proper funding of education. Those countries whose percentages of GDP allocated to education fell below 26 percent had underfunding of education, while those countries whose percentages of GDP allocated to education fell below 15 percent had poor funding of education.

Fundamental Indices responsible for Underfunding of Education in Developing Countries

The Economy

The economy is a major determinant of proper financing of education because of its structural functionalism. If the structural functionalism of an economy is capital-drive oriented, the country involved will adequately finance education, unlike an economy that is commodity oriented. For instance, America and Europe have inbuilt regulatory mechanisms, and these make their economies viable and stable. Developing countries such as Nigeria and other African countries do not have an inbuilt regulatory mechanism, hence the fluctuations and instability.

It is equally pertinent to stress that distortion in monetary and fiscal policies has also brought the potency of economies of developing countries to deplorable levels, and this has resulted in the devaluation of currency, thus leading to cuts in the education vote.

Allocable Mechanism Among the Three Tiers of Government

A peep into the allocable mechanism in developing countries revealed that most of them have not been able to meet the UNESCO's 26 percent allocable mechanism to education. Several reasons explain the above statement:

- In the advanced countries of the world, educational finance is influenced by the rate of returns analysis.

That is, those who benefit more pay more for acquiring education. In the developing countries of the world, because of social welfare functions, education is heavily shouldered by the government. For example, to reduce illiteracy rate in a developing country, government shoulders financing of education.

- National income and per capita income are higher in advanced countries than in developing countries.
- In advanced countries, the enrollment is being lowered, but in the developing countries, enrollment is being accumulated.

Political Instability

Paradoxically, most developing countries—including Nigeria—have not been able to enjoy the dividends of democracy in the last two decades as a result of military rule and political instability. The most negative aspect of this is the fluctuation in education policy making. In the last one decade, for example, Nigeria has moved from UPE to UBE without appropriate policy guidelines and coordination in the removal of the appointed coordinators of the programs.

Governments' Misplaced Priorities

This is another contributory factor to underfunding of education in the developing countries. The governments' misplaced priorities in other sectors of the economy have rendered the education sector impotent as far as funding is concerned.

Effects of Underfunding on Education

Inadequate Physical Structures and Facilities

Inadequate physical structures and facilities occasioned by school population explosion, and dwindling financial resources have turned educational policy goals to unattainable. In the words of Obikoya (2002), "Many lecture theatres are in a state of disrepair, halls of residence are wearing with leaking dilapidated roofs. Electricity, water and access roads are in short supply and science laboratories are poorly equipped. Available classroom buildings can no longer be maintained . . . Thus, in many schools, students are seen standing outside the classrooms to receive lectures through the windows" (45). This problem is making it difficult to actualize the aspirations of the country, which the education sector is to bring.

Hampered Academic Programs

Though tertiary institutions are designed to foster scholarship and research for the development of the country, it is quite unfortunate that most tertiary institutions now find it difficult to attend international workshops and conferences due to scarcity of funds. Worse still, some of them find it difficult to obtain funds for running cost from the government. All these hamper the goals of these institutions for the country. This same problem is applicable to primary and secondary schools. The teachers are no more attending workshops, seminars, and conferences that will keep them abreast of new innovations in teaching technology because of inadequate funding of education.

Constraints to National Development

Development of a country is a function of human capital that the education sector produces. Educational funds should be conditioned by human capital principle; this explains why more money should be allocated to education sector than all other sectors of the economy. Developing countries such as Nigeria and other African countries cannot expect sound output in terms of human capital, which is instrumental to national development when education is underfunded. Once there is no correlation between demand and supply of funds to education sector, inefficiency of investment will set in. Thus, the development of the country in all facets is being jeopardized, and this explains why the country's pursuit of technological advancement is a mirage.

Other Effects of Educational Underfunding

Other effects of education underfunding are poor academic performance, a lower commitment to work, human capital flight, and preference for private jobs among teachers.

Strategies for Raising Additional Resources for Education

For a variety of reasons, education in developing countries is facing growing financial constraints. As a result, more effort is being put into research and analysis of alternative methods of financing education, particularly the cost recovery and the distribution of the financial burden of investing in education (Adedeji, 2002).

The World Bank (1980) stresses that the increasing demands of education on public finance at a time when government funds are stagnant or even falling in many developing countries can only be resolved by either finding additional sources of financial support or reducing unit costs through greater efficiency. To this end, this section has identified the following strategies for additional sources of financial support for education using Nigeria as an example.

Repositioning the Economy from Mono-directional to Multidirectional

Provision of additional sources of financial support for education is a function of dynamic economy. Samuel (2002) emphasizes that as the level of capital formation is low while enrollments at all levels continue to increase astronomically, the economy will not be able to rise to the occasion. There is a need, therefore, to reposition the Nigerian economy from a monolith to a multidirectional economy by exploring and expanding other sectors of the economy apart from crude oil. Agricultural sector that was the mainstay of the economy in 1970s needs to be revitalized. Energy and gas need to be explored and expanded. Industrialization and tourism will energize the country's financial muscle if they are adequately encouraged. All these will go a long way to improve the GDP, the GNI, and the per capita income, which will enable the government and households to have additional financial resources to efficiently and effectively fund education.

Reintroduction of Tuition Fees in Schools as a Matter of National Policy

The government should go back to the recommendation of the Longe Commission. The commission recommended that, "As a result of the gross deterioration and dilapidation of facilities in the institutions, payment of fees by students in federal institutions should be restored as an exercise in the partial recovery of cost" (Ukeje 2002:23). The policy of free education at all levels has already been neglected by the government. This is evident in a recent study conducted by the World Bank on education expenditure in Nigeria in which the unit cost for households at primary and secondary levels was N33,000 and N42,000 respectively, while that of the government was under N3,000 for primary and less than N1,000 for secondary in Lagos State (Samuel 2002). Government should come out of its shell fully and make a bold step of reintroducing fees in schools rather than hiding under a policy statement that will not be implemented.

Strict Adherence to the Principle of Prime Beneficiary

In a paper presented at the forum on cost and financing education in Nigeria sponsored by the World Bank in September 2002, Professor Tunde Samuel advocated the principle of prime beneficiary for raising additional financial resources for education in Nigeria. According to him, "He who takes the lion's share of the benefits of education must bear the biggest cost. in essence, if parents and their wards or government reap more benefits from education, the cost and financing of education should tilt heavily towards them"

Policies on the funding of education should be in line with the principles of prime beneficiary . This principle is what the advanced countries such as United States and Britain are adopting towards funding education.

Diversification of Reasonable Percentage of Alumni Fees to Capital Projects

Alumni associations are a major source of funding in some parts of the world, particularly in the United States. Where they are well organized, they make regular annual donations to their schools (Ukeje 2002). In the same vein, as a matter of policy, alumni associations should channel a reasonable percentage of alumni fees being collected annually from graduating students towards financing some capital projects in their various institutions. This will relieve the financial burdens on the governments and on the institutions.

Private Sector Participation in Funding Education

The government should mandate private institutions such as Chevron, Julius Berger, United African Company UAC, banks, and other multinational companies to assist in funding through the provision of welfare services to the schools. They can also award more scholarships and bursary to brilliant and indigent students who cannot afford school fees.

Chapter Nine

A Technique of Educational Project Time Analysis

The complexity of the school as an organization has developed to the extent whereby the employment of administrative methods, based mainly on personal traits of leadership is inadequate for the achievement of its objectives. Effective management of any industry requires efficient planning and implementation of program to meet its goals. The education industry, like other industries, has a goal that must be accomplished efficiently and effectively with the available resources. The educational system has come to realization that its survival in the midst of scarce resources will depend on how well the available resources are maximally utilized within the time frame. Hence, the need for the adoption of management techniques in project time analysis by the head, the staff, and those involved in the education enterprise to ensure the effectiveness and efficiency of the school system. One of these management techniques is program evaluation and review technique (PERT).

Program Evaluation and Review Technique

PERT is a method being used to analyze the tasks involved in competing a given project, especially the time needed to complete each task and to identify the minimum time needed to complete the total project.

This model was invented by Booz Allen Hamilton and was used on a large scale by the United States Navy Department in 1958 for controlling the development progress of the Submarine Launched Ballistic Missiles (SLBMs) project. The navy program involved several subcomponent projects, which by their nature were complex and needed a model that could help control and coordinate the several activities of the 3,000 contractors working on different aspects of the program (Buffa 1975).

PERT became an invaluable means of planning the sequence of events. It acts as a manager's tool for defining and coordinating what must be done to accomplish the objectives of a project on time successfully. PERT is based on the theory of graph, and it is expressed in graphic diagrams in the form of a network of arrows resulting from the analysis of a program. These diagrams support the elements used to establish the calculations. It follows from this definition that in order to introduce the general principles on which the PERT method is based, it is necessary to consider the program analysis phase and the phase of constructing the network and the significance of these different elements.

Program Analysis

Analysis consists of specifying the precise objectives of the program and breaking them down into successive stages. The task, therefore, is to define a general objective of the program and subdivide it into partial objectives or successive phases of advancement. In brief, program analysis tries to provide answers to the following questions:

1. What is the objective and what is the starting point towards achieving it?
2. What are the major intermediate events to be achieved in order to carry out the program?
3. What activities are necessary to achieve these events?

Analysis, therefore, amounts to defining the key points of the program, that is to say, its origin, its objective, its events, and the activities to be carried out.

Networking brings out the relationships of defined objectives. It also shows various degrees of complexity for each degree of responsibility.

Some Fundamental Terms and Symbols used in PERT Network Construction

An Event

This is the beginning or end of a task. It is a point that marks the start or completion of a task. It does not consume any time, money, or effort. Events must take place in a logical sequence. That is, event A must follow B, and C must follow D, and so on. An event is represented in a network by a circle.

An Activity

This refers to the actual performance of a task or work, and it must link two consecutive events in the PERT network. On this basis, a PERT activity requires some effort and time to be accomplished. That is, the PERT activity consumes time, requires resources, and can be understood as representing the time, effort, and resources required to move from one event to another. A PERT activity cannot be completed until the event preceding it has occurred.

A Network

This refers to a series of interested and interdependent activities and events that when performed, will yield some products or services that invariably contribute to the attainment of the overall goals of an organization.

A network is essentially the graphic representation of the logical structure of the project to be executed and shows the relationship between the events and activities that constitute the project. Geometrically, the network consists of two elements: events and activities.

The diagram below shows events and activities.

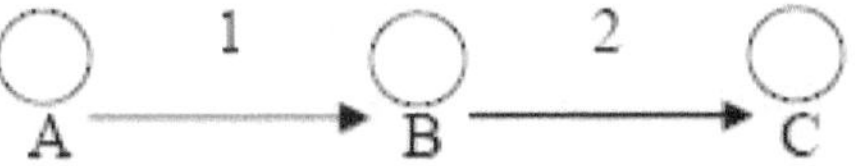

A, B, and C are events, while 1 and 2 are the activities. Events are represented by circles and activities are represented by arrows joining two or more events following the direction of a lapse of time.

Hints on Construction of PERT Network

1. Break down the project (task) into events and activities.
2. Allocate time to each activity since activities are the time consuming portions of the PERT network.
3. Subject the time so allocated to time estimates using the PERT network formula

   $$t_e = \frac{O + 4M + P}{6}$$

   Where t = expected time, O = optimistic time, M = most likely time, and P = pessimistic time.

4. Construct the network beginning with the events.
5. Construct and show all items.
6. Work out the latest allowable time and finally compute the slack.

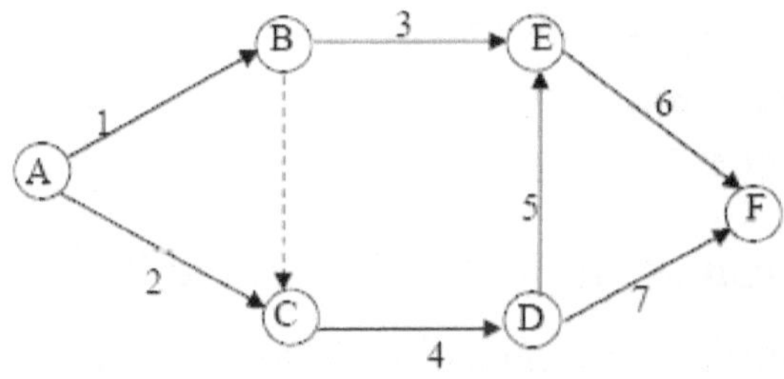

O = event / - - - - - ▶ Dummy activity / ——▶ activity

Dummy activity refers to the activity that does not require any time, effort or resources for its accomplishment.

Time Scheduling in PERT

In constructing PERT network, it is important to work out the time schedule for completion of the project. Three time estimates are usually involved.

The Optimistic Time

This is the minimum possible period of time in which a task can be accomplished, assuming everything proceeds better than it is normally expected. It is denoted by the symbol O in the formula.

The Most Likely Time

This is the best estimate of the time in which a task can be accomplished, assuming everything proceeds as it was originally scheduled. It is denoted by the symbol M in the formula.

The Pessimistic Time

This is the maximum possible period it would take to accomplish a task, assuming everything goes wrong, but excluding major catastrophies or setbacks. It is denoted by the symbol P in the formula.

These three time estimates are stated in days, weeks, or months. The estimates represent calendar days. From these three time estimates, the expected time (t_e) for the completion of each activity using the formula can be computed.

Note: $t_e = (O + 4M + P)/6$. t_e is the average time the activity would consume.

Computation of the Expected Time (T_e)

Expected time (T_e) is the time it would take to reach the next event. It represents the earliest possible time that the event can be reached, and it is computed by adding the t_e's of the activity along the paths leading to the event. Time to reach event A is zero; no activity is before it; therefore, no time can be consumed in reaching it.

Latest allowable Completion Time

T_L is the latest allowable completion time for each event. To compute T_L start from the last event and work back towards the first event. Then subtract the value of small t_e from the value of T_E for the successor event.

Slack

The slack of an event is the latest allowable time minus the expected time. $S = T_L - T_E$

Exercises

The table below provides time estimates related to the various activities on the project for the building of science laboratory in a senior secondary school.

		Time Estimates (months)		
Activity	Description	O	M	P
A – B	Invitation of tenders	5	10	12
B – C	Screening and approving of contractors	2	3	15
B – D	Taking contractors to the site	2	6	10
C – E	Site clearing	1	2	3
D – E	Dummy Activity	-	-	-
D – F	Purchase of Materials	4	5	9
E – G	Construction Started	4	6	11
F – G	Construction/Installation/ Fittings completed	4	6	8

Questions

1. Calculate the t_e (expected time) for each activity.
2. Construct a network model for the project.
3. Calculate for each event: (1) T_E (ii) T_L and (iii) S.

Solutions

1. Expected time for each event (t_e)

		Time Estimates (months)			Expected Time
Activity	Description	O	M	P	Te=O+4M+P/6
A – B	Invitation of tenders	5	10	12	9.5
B – C	Screening and approving of contractors	2	3	15	4.8
B – D	Taking contractors to the site	2	6	10	6.0
C – E	Site clearing	1	2	3	2.0
D – E	Dummy activity	-	-	-	-
D – F	Purchase of materials	4	5	9	5.5
E – G	Construction started	4	6	11	6.5
F – G	Construction/ installation fittings completed	4	6	8	6.0

2. A Network Model for the Project

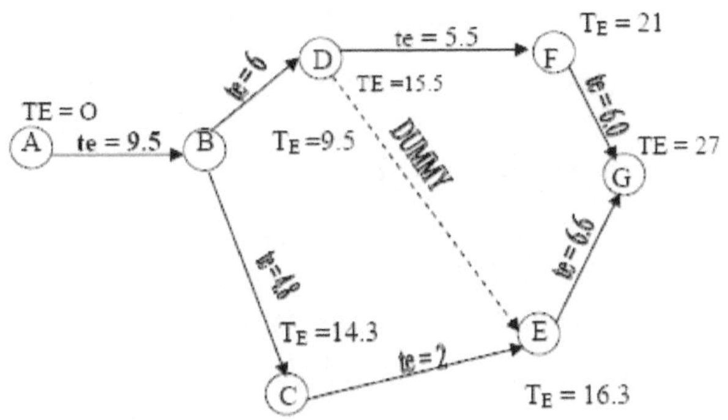

3. The PERT Network for the construction of a Science Laboratory in a Senior Secondary School.

3a. T_E for each event

The T_E for event A = O

T_E for event B = (O + 9.5) = 9.5 months

T_E for event C = (9.5 + 4.8) = 14.3 months

T_E for event D = (9.5 + 6) = 15.5 months

T_E for event E = (14.3 + 2) = 16.3 months

T_E for event F = (15.5 + 5.5) = 21 months

T_E for event G = (21 + 6.0) = 27 months

* All these (T_E's) are shown in the network constructed above.

3b. T_L for each event

T_L for event A = O

T_L for event B = (9.5 – 9.5) = 0

T_L for event C = (14.3 – 4.8) = 9.5

T_L for event D = (15.5 – 6) = 9.5

T_L for event E = (16.3 – 2) = 14.3

T_L for event F = (21 – 5.5) = 15.5

T_L for event G + (27 – 6.0) = 21

Slack for each event ($T_L - T_E$)

S for event A (T_L = O, T_E = O); O – O = O
S for event B (T_L = 9.5, T_E = 9.5); 9.5 – 9.5 = O
S for event C (T_L = 9.5, T_E = 14.3); 9.5 – 14.3 = 14.8
S for event D (T_L = 9.5, T_E = 15.5); 9.5 – 15.5 = - 6
S for event E (T_L = 14.2, T_E = 16.2); 14.3 – 16.2 = - 2
S for event F (T_L = 15.5, T_E = 21); 15.5 – 21 = - 5.5
S for event G (T_L = 21, T_E = 27); 21 – 27 = - 6

Notes

1. If the slack is positive, it means that there are more than enough resources to execute the project.
2. If the slack is negative, it is an indication of behind schedule condition in which case the resources are not enough.
3. If the slack is zero, it is an indication that there are just enough resources to execute the project.

The value of slack determines how critical an event is. The concept of slack is important as it provides planners and administrators a measure of flexibility for the scheduling of their activities, the allocation of available resources and for ensuring that the projected production rate of an organization is maintained.

References

Abagi, Okwachi. *Public and Private Investment in Education in Kenya: An Agenda for Action.* IPAR Publication, 2002.

Adedeji, S.O. "Cost and Financing of Education in Nigeria: The Historical Perspective." *Education Today,* 10, no. 1 (2002): 17–26.

Aigbokhan, B., O. J. Imahe, and M. I. Ailemen. "Education Expenditure and Human Capital Development in Nigeria: Any Correlation So Far?" http://www.regional-studies-assoc.ac.uk (accessed 2007).

Akinyemi, S. "The Analysis of Unit Cost of Public Primary Education in Lagos State (1998–2003)." Unpublished Ph.D. thesis, Lagos State University, 2005.

Akinyemi, S. T. *Some Socio-Economic Issues in Nigeria 1.* Lagos: Center for Educational Aid, 1999.

Appleton, S. and F. Teal. "Human Capital and economic development. The African Development Report" http://www.accenture.com/global/researchandinsights, 1998 (accessed December 18, 2007).

Babalola, J. B. *Educational Costs and Financing Analysis.* External Studies Program, University of Ibadan, 1992.

Borthwick, S. "Overview of Student Costs and Government funding in Post-Compulsory Education and Training." *Research and Evaluation Branch Report* 4, no. 99 (1999): 20–28.

Coombs, P. H. and J. Hallak. *Cost Analysis in Education: A Tool for Policy and Planning.* London: The Johns Hopkins University Press, 1987.

Encyclopedia of the Third World Vol. 2. City: Publisher, 1978.

Federal Government of Nigeria Decree No. 7, 1993.

Federal Ministry of Education. *National Policy on Education,* 4th ed. Lagos: NERDC Press, 2004.

Finer, S. E. *Comparative Government: An Introduction to the Study of Politics*.London: Heinnman Lo: Publisher, 1969.

Hietala, K. *Human Capital: General Framework for Long-Term Social Impact Evaluation of Employment Strategy*. http://ec-europa.eu/employment (accessed 2003).

Hill, K., D. Hoffman, and T. R. Rex. *The Value of Higher Education: Individual and Societal Benefits.* Arizona L. William Seidman Research Institute. http://wcpcarey.asu.edu/scid/upload/value %20 report final October %202005a.pdf (accessed 2005).

Lucy, R. *Return to Education.* London: Elsevier Scientific Publishing Company, 1980.

Madumere, C. O. *Statistical Tools to Educational Management Problems in Developing Countries.* Lagos: Joja Press Limited, 1989.

Mitha, N. J., K. Njogu, K. Ngela, and A. Madha. *Cost and Financing of Education in Kenya: Access, Quality and Equality in Primary Education.* Nairobi: The World Bank and Ministry of Education, 1995.

Mureithi, L. and C. Wasikama. *Human Resources Development in Africa; A Strategic Factor in Claiming Africa's Future.* http://unpani.un.org/intradoc/group/public/document, (accessed 2000).

O'Donoghue, M. *Economic Dimension in Education.* Dublin: Gill and Macmillan Limited, 1971.

Ogbodo, C. M. "Financing in Nigeria." *Introduction to Educational Administration, Planning, and Supervision.* Edited by V. F. Peretomode. Lagos: Joja Publishers, 1995.

Oguntoye, A. O. and R. A. Alani. *Financing Education in Nigeria: Theory and Practices*. Ilaro: Kinsbond Investment Limited, 1998.

Oyedeji, L. *The UPE in Nigeria: Its Implication for National Development*. Lagos: Univesrity of Lagos Press, 1983.

Population Reference Bureau. "Population and Economic Development Linkages: 2007 Data Sheet." Washington DC: Brigde, 2007.

Price Water House Coppers. *The Economic Benefits of Higher Education*. Institute of Physics. http://www.rsc.org/education/policy/economicsofhighereducation.asp (accessed 2003).

Samuel, T. "Cost-Benefit Analysis and Investment Decision Making in Education: A System Analysis of the Nigerian Situation." *Educational Perspective,* 2 no. 1 (1990): 119–126.

Samuel, T. "Strategies for Raising Additional Resources for Education." *Education Today,* 10 no. 1 (2003): 40–43.

Samuel, T. (1994). "Underfunding of Education in Nigeria: A Micro-Economic Explanation." *Journal of Applied Research in Education*, 2 no. 1 (1994): 81–85.

Sexton, J. and J. Hall. (2000). "Investment in Education: Private and Public Returns." Joint Economic Committee Study. http://www.house.gov/jec/edu/htm (accessed 2000).

Small, M. "Inflation and the International Monetary Situation." *Journal of American Economic Association*, 2 no. 1 (1967): 23–26.

Stroombergen, A., R. Dennis, and G. Nana. (2002). "Review of the Statistical Measurement of Human Capital." *Statistics New Zealand.* http://www.stats.govt.nz (accessed 2002).

Umo, J. "Reinventing Human Capital as Answers to Multiple Questions." *The Guardian* (January 13, 1998): 9.

United Nations International Children's Emergency Fund Report, 1995.

Walker, I. and Y. Zhu. "Education, Earning and Productivity: A Recent UK Evidence." shttp://statistics.gov.uk/articles/labormarkettrends/education.pdf (accessed 2003).

www.ingramcontent.com/pod-product-compliance
Lightning Source LLC
Chambersburg PA
CBHW030727210726
48505CB00028B/318

* 9 7 8 1 6 1 2 0 4 2 0 0 8 *